Bearing True Witness

(or, "Now That I've Found Islam, What Do I Do With It?")

DR. LAURENCE B. BROWN, MD

Copyright

Reprinting

Translating

Website

Introduction

One of the first lessons I learned as a new author was to narrow the subject of my books, and define the audience for which they were written. Hence, the dream of one book grew into the reality of two, with a third planned to complete the trilogy.

This present book is the second in the series.

The first book in this series was written to guide those seeking the religion of truth. This first book, entitled *The First and Final Commandment* (Amana publications; website www.amana-publications.com), argues the continuity of revelation from Judaism to Christianity, and then to Islam.

This present book -- the second in the trilogy -- provides guidance in the practical aspects of the Islamic religion, and is intended for converts and for those Muslims who seek to clarify their religion.

The third book in the series is in the planning stage, as of the date of this writing, but is intended to address the many disingenuous criticisms and blatant slanders leveled against Muslims and the Islamic religion. Topics such as polygamy, slavery, racism, the female headscarf, oppression of women, terrorism, "fundamentalism," idolatry and others are to be discussed with similar methodology to that employed in *The First and Final Commandment*.

The order of this series of books, then, is to present the Islamic religion as the final revelation and fulfillment of predictions of the Jewish and Christian scriptures in the first book, to suggest the manner in which the Islamic religion should be practically applied in the second, and to provide the confirmed Muslim with defense against the most common slanders against Islam in the third.

Regarding the present work, Muslims frequently observe that converts to the Islamic religion progress through several stages of ideological, spiritual, and psychological growth before achieving a semblance of religious maturity. The period of maturation varies from one individual to another, as does the end result. Some Muslims have shown remarkable religious maturity as children. Others experience dramatic reversal of ideology late in life. The renunciation of extreme Sufism by the famous eleventh century (CE) Imam Al-Ghazali (full name: Abu Haamid Muhammad Al-Ghazali) in later life, and the refutation of his errors in *aqeeda* by the tenth century (CE) Al-Ash'aree (full name: Abu Al-Hasan 'Ali ibn Ismaa'eel al-Ash'aree, to whom the Ash'aree *aqeeda* is attributed), also late in his days, serve as prominent examples. In more recent history, Malcolm X's transition from the racist and ideologically condemned political cult known as the Nation of Islam to orthodox (Sunni) Islam is perhaps the best known example.

In the beginning, Muslim converts frequently embark upon widely divergent ideological paths on the grayscale that spans the gap between the clear purity of

3

correctness and the murky darkness of deviation. Although many eventually settle upon the path of Islamic correctness, a large number also become confirmed upon degrees of deviancy, sometimes of such a mild degree as to warrant naught but advice, occasionally of such magnitude as to warrant punishment according to the *Shari'a* (Islamic law), and all too often of such severity as to invalidate a person's *shahada* (testimony of faith) entirely, meaning that the person in question, whether knowingly or not, invalidates their claim to being Muslim and leaves the religion of Islam.

For the individual, the importance of correctness of religious path relates to salvation. For the community, the importance relates to the errors of the deviants misrepresenting, and hence creating misunderstanding of, the Islamic religion as a whole.

The author, being a Western convert to the Islamic religion, has lived the heedless hedonism that accompanies absence of religion, the awakening of spiritual awareness in the heart of the seeker, the soulful search for truth, the cautious sifting of religions for ingredients of value and consistency, the serenity of embrace of truth when found, and times both pleasant and unpleasant following and at all points in the process. Having lived and worked as a Muslim in the Western countries of America and England, and subsequently in the Holy City of Medina Al-Munawara has conferred a depth of experience that may be of interest to those who seek a similar path.

Nonetheless, what follows is not a book of memoirs, but rather of analysis. The fact is that the presented issues have been analyzed by Islamic scholars since the time of revelation, and the correct path for each issue has been defined since the time of the last messenger, Muhammad ibn Abdullahﷺ. The paucity of information available in the English language, however, results in many Western converts being ill-informed and, as consequence, easily mislead.

The information that follows is the author's best attempt at rectifying that unfortunate situation.

4

1) The Commitment

The choice having been made, a person enters Islam and becomes Muslim with the *shahada*, or testimony of faith. This testimony (transliterated from Arabic) reads, "*Ash-hadu an la ilaha illa Llah(u), wa ash-hadu anna Muhammad an Rasulu Llah,*" and is translated, "I testify that there is no god (also translated, 'there is no object worthy of worship') but Allah and I testify that Muhammadﷺ is the Messenger of Allah."

The *shahada* is most traditionally stated in public, for in general, converts should let their conversion be known. However, should the situation necessitate it, the *shahada* may be stated with none other than The Creator for witness.

The *shahada* not only affirms divine unity and the prophethood of Muhammad ibn Abdullahﷺ, but also commits the faithful to all that is enjoined by the religion, and to abstain from all that is forbidden. Hence, although the statement says nothing about prohibition against fornication, adultery, alcohol, etc., acceptance of these prohibitions is inextricably coupled with the *shahada*. For to accept Muhammadﷺ as a prophet, and for that matter, as the final prophet, mandates acceptance of the message and laws that were revealed through him. Anything less is hypocrisy.

The first duty of a convert, then, is to fully understand the meaning of the *shahada*, and begin to live it.[1] Many excellent books have been written on this subject, and there is little or no point in duplicating previous works, although a brief outline is perhaps in order. To begin with, the commitment of greatest and most obvious importance when stating the *shahada* is the recognition of monotheism (i.e., the oneness of Allah, which is captured in the Arabic language by the term *tawheed*). This point cannot be stressed too strongly. Islam is the religion of *tawheed*. Any compromise to Islamic monotheism, any compromise to the supremacy and absolute Oneness of Allah constitutes *shirk*. *Shirk* exists in varying degrees, from major *shirk*, which takes a person out of Islam, to minor *shirk*, which ranks as a major sin, to *riyaa*, or hidden *shirk*. Examples of major *shirk* are to worship other than Allah or to join partners in worship with Allah. Examples of minor *shirk* include swearing an oath by other than Allah or trusting to 'good luck' charms. Lastly, examples of hidden *shirk* are to beautify a person's prayer when aware that someone else is watching, or to give more in charity than a person would otherwise when aware that the donation is being observed. Given the critical importance of these partner subjects of *tawheed* and *shirk*, further study in books devoted to these subjects is strongly recommended.[2]

Subsidiary to *tawheed* is declaration of Muhammadﷺ as the final prophet and messenger of Islam – an acknowledgement of particular importance due to the fact that so many messianic pretenders have advanced false claims of prophethood over the years, misguiding masses down diverse paths of deviancy in the process. Elijah Poole Muhammad, the founder of the Nation of Islam, is but one such example. Others of his misguided and misguiding breed include Mizra Ghulam Ahmad, the

---

[1] Scholars teach that the *shahada* is not valid without seven elements: knowledge, sincerity, honesty, love of the *shahada*, certainty, abstention from anything that negates the *shahada*, and application (or, in other words, to live the testimony of faith).
[2] Such books are readily available online through a variety of Islamic bookstores

founder of the Ahmadiyyah (also known as the Qadianis), *Bab* Mirza Ali Muhammad and Mirza Husain Ali (the founders of the Baha'i) and a plethora of other colorful and peculiar, but influential, messianic pretenders to have surfaced over the past 1,400 years. Acknowledgement of Muhammadﷺ as the final prophet of Allah closes the door of the mind to consideration of the claims of all such messianic pretenders. Furthermore, the completion of the chain of prophethood through the person of Muhammad ibn Abdullahﷺ is consistent with predictions of previous scripture (for fuller explanation, the reader is referred to *The First and Final Commandment*, the first book in this series).

Finally, implicit in the declaration of the *shahada* is acceptance of the fundamentals of Islamic faith (known as 'pillars,' for without these pillars of faith and practice, a person's commitment to the religion collapses). Any mainstream Islamic bookstore catalogs several books which define these pillars of Islamic faith and practice. From small pamphlets to extensive tomes, available books range from the superficial to the scholastic. In brief, the essential articles of faith are six: belief in Allah, His angels, the revealed scriptures, the messengers, the Hereafter, and Divine decree. The required duties of worship are five: declaration of faith upon entry into the religion (i.e., *shahada*), prayer five times daily (at prescribed intervals, and in accordance with the rules of prayer and purification), annual fasting of the month of Ramadan, annual payment of the poor-due, and pilgrimage to Mecca during the period of *Haj*, once in a lifetime, if physically and financially able.

So that's it! Just say the *shahada*, adopt the beliefs and practices, and you're on your way. Easy, right? Weeeeeeell, yes, but no. If there is one point of overbearing importance that needs to be conveyed to new Muslims, it is this: Islam is a religion of structure. Every tenet, every teaching, every belief and every valid element of the Islamic religion has a basis in revealed reality. When a Muslim tells another something in the Islamic religion, he or she needs to be able to support that teaching with Islamic evidence. The gold standard (and for that matter, the only accepted standard) of Islamic legitimization is to be found in the interpretation of Islamic evidences by those of comprehensive knowledge (i.e., Muslim scholars). And what are the sources of Islamic evidences? Two -- the revealed word of Allah (i.e., the Holy Qur'an), and the Sunnah (literally 'the way' of the prophet Muhammad ibn Abdullahﷺ, meaning his teachings and example, as conveyed through his words, actions, appearance and implied consents, as preserved in the Islamic traditions known as *hadith*). So in the end, every valid teaching has a foundation in the Islamic evidences, and like it or not, that evidence must be clear, present, and substantiated in order for any specific teaching to be considered acceptable.

So when learning from another Muslim, whether beloved or not, respected or dis-, credentialed or un-, the critical question for each and every teacher regarding each and every teaching is simply, "Where did you get that?" If from the individual's mind, watch out! For it was by this slippery path of caprice and opinion that previous masses were led astray. Other pathways to error include:

1. Mysticism. Now, let's dwell on this issue for a moment. Piety and righteousness is expected to lead to a certain level of enhanced insight and understanding of things religious. But while there is nothing wrong with seeking such enlightenment, believers go astray when they

try too hard and, in the process, leave the rules of guidance dictated by The Creator for rules defined by a human being such as, for example, a mystic. And this is the most critical indication of deviation into mysticism – the embracing of teachings and practices that are not founded upon valid sources of Islamic law, which is to say the Qur'an, Sunnah, and the interpretation thereof by respected Sunni scholars. When unfounded teachings are encountered in combination with spiritual leaders who brandish self-aggrandizing claims of enhanced spiritual insight, by which they justify their bizarre and unfounded beliefs and/or practices, the situation should be obvious. Too often, however, it is not, for many of the misguiding deviants quote Qur'an and Sunnah to support their astray beliefs. The fact that these deviants *mis*quote or *mis*interpret Qur'an and draw upon *un*authentic hadith in support of their position frequently goes unnoticed by those lacking the intellectual tools by which to differentiate correctly interpreted, authentic sources from manipulated and/or unauthentic sources. Please see chapter 5, entitled 'Sufism,' for further discussion of this subject. Still more pathways to error include:

2. Philosophy (for the philosophers are not in agreement with one another, so at most only one group can be right. And while on the subject, look at what happened to the Greeks!)

3. Rationalism (for not everything in religion 'makes sense' to everybody, and the inclination to discard or modify religious standards simply because a person can't 'make sense' of them leads to deviancy and, not infrequently, disbelief. Typically, attempts to rationalize deviant viewpoints are the result of people seeking to modify the religion to match their desires, with attempts to 'modernize' or 'adapt' Islam being classic examples.)

4. Over-intellectualization (Muslims are expected to think and reason, not only in order to arrive at belief in the first place, but also in order to practice and apply the religion correctly. However, intellectualization has practical limits, meaning that there are some things people simply have to accept, believe, and do – things like, for example, the commands of Allah. Should people refuse to accept, validate, or fulfill a command of Allah, simply because they can't understand the reason for it, they fall into disobedience and error.)

5. False justification (such as through misquoting or misinterpreting Qur'anic verses, or employing weak or fabricated hadith in order to support a deviant position)

6. Passing judgment on an issue despite lacking scholastic qualification.

However, if guidance is taken from respected and qualified scholars who derive their teachings from the Holy Qur'an and authentic hadith, then a person can rest at ease.

Lacking substantiation by qualified scholars, in accordance with foundational evidences from Qur'an and Sunnah, no people should consider themselves safe. When the map of history is reviewed, mankind is found to have strayed whenever the halter of human intellect was torn from the hand of supportive evidences and turned loose in the field of enticing explanations. The search of the alchemists for the 'philosopher's stone' (the mythical formula by which base metals could be transmuted to gold), for the fountain of immortality, for the pots of gold and dreams conceived in every legend that ever launched a ship or expedition on a venture of futility are easy examples. Yet no baseless legends have ever led to the frivolous sacrifice of more wealth, energy, lives and souls than those of false religion.

The First and Final Commandment betrays the weak, nonexistent, or frankly fabricated foundation of many of the myths of modern Judaic and Christian theology. Orthodox (Sunni) Islam refuses to accept such hypocrisy within its creed, and maintains the purity of its teachings through requiring scholars to derive the *fiqh* (Islamic laws) from the stable and respected foundational sources of the Islamic religion, and then by requiring the laity to follow the valid decisions of qualified scholars.

Unfortunately, many new converts conceive the supremely optimistic, and sadly naïve, assumption that all 'scholars' know what they are talking about, and that all Muslims are upon the same path. Nothing could be further from the truth. A large variety of sects identify with the label of Islam, all the while ranging in ideological assay anywhere from minor innovation to outright blasphemy. Some heretical sects cling to the sharply defined borders of Islam, whereas others are so far out of the envelope of Islam as to warrant a separate metaphysical mailing code.

Hence, the need for labels.

In general, Muslims prefer to be known as nothing more than, well, *Muslims*, for the simple reason that Allah Most High refers to the believers as Muslims in the Holy Qur'an. For those who revere the supremacy of Allah, no label created in the mind of man can compete with that chosen by the Creator Himself. However, labels have become necessary in order to distinguish between differing groups. The two largest subdivisions in the Islamic world are the Sunnis and the Shi'ites. Sunni Muslims adhere to the *sunnah* (way) of the prophet Muhammad鷺, as conveyed through the Islamic traditions (hadith), whereas the Shi'ites adhere to the teachings of their religious leaders (Imams), whether validated by the Qur'an and Sunnah or not. As typically occurs whenever people give precedence to charismatic leaders over revealed truth, a few peculiar individuals with even more bizarre ideology crept into the chain of authority at various points in history, established their deviancy in the canon of the religion, and distracted the sectarian beliefs, divergent step by divergent step, from the truth of the period of origins. Destructive deviant trends, similar to those that developed in the hearts and minds of the Shi'ites, have effectively cleaved a long list of other sects from the main body of Sunni Muslims.

Nonetheless, Sunni Islam accounts for approximately 95% of all Muslims worldwide, and for good reason. To begin with, the methodology makes sense. Anybody who accepts Islam affirms the supremacy and oneness of Allah, which of necessity negates any concept of partners or co-sharers in divinity. As per the translation of the meaning of the Qur'an (hereafter TMQ),[3]

---

[3]The version of the translation of the meaning of the Qur'an (TMQ) quoted in this book, unless otherwise noted, is *The Qur'an, Arabic Text with Corresponding English Meanings*, by Saheeh International.

9

"So do not attribute to Allah equals while you know (that there is nothing similar to Him)" [TMQ 2:22]

and

"Say, 'He is Allah, (who is) one, Allah, the Eternal Refuge. He neither begets nor is born, Nor is there to Him any equivalent.'" (TMQ 112:1-4).

Hence, there is only one supreme and final authority, and that is Allah, and His choice of the Holy Qur'an as the final revelation and of Muhammad ibn Abdullahﷺ as the final messenger is to be respected. Furthermore, over and again, Allah instructs mankind in the Holy Qur'an to follow the example of the final prophet, and to obey Allah and his messenger, Muhammadﷺ. Once is enough, but the frequent repetition of this teaching by Allah Most High, in His revelation, should dismiss any discussion of this point.

Given the primacy of the example of Muhammadﷺ in the religion of Islam, the dedication and rigor with which previous generations preserved the library of hadith records is legendary. For this reason, there is simply no person in history about whom so much detail is documented and confirmed. Unlike the fuzzy profiles of all previous prophets, the life, character, and teachings of Muhammadﷺ can be known in exquisite detail, and it is this detail to which Sunni Muslims adhere.

In contrast, Shi'ite Muslims are just one group of a long list of deviant sects that have chosen to disregard the Sunnah of Muhammadﷺ, to one degree or another, in favor of the teachings of their sectarian leaders. Similar to the Christians who discarded the orthodox teachings of Christ Jesus in favor of the more permissive, though contrary, theology of Paul, deviant sects of Islam assign priority to human teachings contrary to those based upon Qur'an, Sunnah, and the interpretation thereof by qualified scholars.

Unfortunately (and predictably, as well), many deviants misquote or misinterpret the Qur'an and hadith in order to support their religious misdirection. And unless people question what they are told, some of the evidence that is cited may appear convincing for, as William Shakespeare stated, "The devil can cite Scripture for his purpose."[4]

New converts, who may not know the difference between the orthodox and the deviant, between the pseudoscholar of deviancy and the valid scholar of truth, must be particularly careful to research and confirm what they are told. More importantly, the faithful will pray for Allah to shelter their hearts, minds, bodies and souls from deviation, and to establish and maintain them upon the straight path of His design. And that is, after all, the prayer of Al-Fatiha, the first surah of the Holy Qur'an, and a prayer of such significance and importance that Allah Most High requires recitation of this surah in each rakat of every prayer. So true Muslims should recite this prayer with sincerity and conviction.

Concerning the above discussion, the following books are particularly helpful in navigating the deviations of the Shi'a (Shi'ites), as well as certain other errant sects:

---

[4] Shakespeare, William. *The Merchant of Venice*. I.iii.

1. The Mirage in Iran -- Dr. Abu Ameenah Bilal Philips' translation of Dr. Ahmad al-Afghani's *Sarab fee Iraan,* and

2. The Devil's Deception -- Dr. Abu Ameenah Bilal Philips' translation of Ibn al-Jawzee's *Talbees Iblees.*

1.a.) The Saved Sect

One oft-cited hadith concludes with the teaching that by the end of time Islam would be divided into 73 sects, 72 of which would be in the fire. When asked which would be the saved sect, Muhammad☀replied to the effect, "Those who follow what I am upon today, and my companions."[5]

Some Muslims suggest that the above hadith has a weakness in its chain of narrators, others point out that the sheer number of transmitters render the hadith sound. Either way, the fact is that if the Islamic religion is not already divided into 73 sects, it is well on its way. Several sects of Shi'ites, a growing number of extreme Sufis, the Ansar cult, the Nation of Islam, the Ahmadiyyah (also known as Qadianees), the Koran'ites, and many others present varying profiles of deviancy from the orthodoxy of Sunni Islam. Furthermore, the concept of the saved sect consisting of those who adhere to what the prophet☀and his companions were upon seems a no-brainer to the confirmed believer.

There are, however, those who propose revision of the Islamic religion on the basis of perceived need to modernize Islam in consideration of the social and political changes of the past 1,400 years. Now, Muslims have historically been some of the most progressive people in the world. The industrial revolution of Europe was largely attributed to knowledge and innovations imported from the Muslim world, at a time when the aristocracy of Europe routinely sent their children to study in the universities of Muslim Spain. Muslims excelled in language and linguistics, mechanical, optical and theoretical physics, organic and inorganic chemistry, mathematics, agriculture, medicine, geography, and astronomy, to name a few of the sciences and arenas of intellect. Many of the technological advances that paved the way for a better world were invented by Muslims, and the university itself originates from the Muslim design of the higher educational institution.[6]

So Muslims are not shy to address the issues of their existence and change with the times in matters that do not conflict with religious principles. However, Allah most High conveyed the teaching through His final prophet, Muhammad☀, that He would not accept any change or innovation in religion. As per the hadith of Aa'ishah, Muhammad☀was recorded as having taught,

> "Whoever innovates anything into this affair of ours [i.e., Islam] that does not belong to it, will have it rejected."[7]

So whereas innovation in matters of non-religious practicality may be praiseworthy, there is no room for innovation in religion itself, for all religious innovations lead to the Hellfire. Remembering that mankind was not created but to serve and worship Allah (see TMQ 51:56; "And I did not create the jinn and mankind except to worship Me."), sense can be made of this formula, for the idea is not to make each and every

---

[5] Tirmidhi (2641)

[6] For further information, please see the first book in this series, *The First and Final Commandment*, chapter 3.C.8, and *Islam and Science*, by Shabir Ahmed, Anas Abdul Muntaqim, and Abdul-Sattar Siddiq; published by the Islamic Cultural Workshop, P.O. Box 1932, Walnut, CA 91789; (909) 399-4708.

[7] Bukhari (2550), Muslim (1718), Sunan Abu Dawud (4606), Ahmad (26075, 26372)

aspect of life easier and more fun, but rather to improve the practicalities of life to facilitate the one duty for which mankind was created -- to serve and worship Allah.

Hence, making life easier in terms of worldly existence is commendable, for it improves the human condition and frees the individual, both physically and mentally, for worship. Physically, improved circumstances make it easier to perform acts of worship, whereas mentally, better conditions give an individual more to be thankful to Allah for. On the other hand, attempting to make religion easier by way of compromising religious duties is blameworthy, for in doing so the individual cheats Allah of the duties for which he or she was created in the first place. Hence, a telephone is better than a carrier pigeon, but whereas four prayers a day is easier than five, it is most definitely not better, for any innovation that conflicts with the Islamic Shari'a (law) deviates from the religion, and rather than making the practice of the religion easier, compromises or destroys it.

Which brings us to a general guiding principle the new Muslim would do well to remember, and that is that everything of worship (meaning everything for which the worshipper expects reward from Allah Most High) is forbidden except that which is prescribed, whereas everything of worldly matters is permitted except that which has been forbidden. This principle is agreed upon by the scholars, and all Muslims should cement it in their memories for the reason that it simplifies the religion and facilitates the decision-making process. Supportive evidence for this principle is so extensive as to be beyond listing in a work such as this, however it should be mentioned that Allah Most High conveyed, in one of the last *ayah* (plural of *ayat*) to be revealed, "This day I have perfected for you your religion and completed My favor upon you and have approved for you Islam as religion" (TMQ 5:3). Taking this *ayat* into consideration along with Allah's oft-repeated mandate to "Obey Allah and His messenger (i.e., Muhammadﷺ)," a Muslim should respect the hadith that relate Muhammadﷺ as having taught,

1. "He who innovates something in this matter (i.e., religion) of ours that is not of it will have it rejected."[8]
2. "What I have forbidden to you, avoid, and what I have ordered you [to do], do as much of it as you can."[9]
3. "Allah, the Exalted, prescribed religious duties, so do not neglect them; He has set boundaries, so no not over-step them; He has prohibited some things, so do not violate them; about some things He was silent – out of compassion for you, not forgetfulness – so seek not after them.*"[10]

---

[8] Bukhari (as a chapter heading entitled: If a civil servant or a judge rules something indifferent to the rule of the messenger, then his rule is rejected) and Muslim (1718)
[9] Bukhari (6858) and Muslim (130)
* Meaning not to delve into those issues upon which Allah, out of His Wisdom and Compassion, withheld ruling, for the answer might bring more distress than benefit. In this regard Allah revealed in the Holy Qur'an, "O you who have believed, do not ask about things which, if they are shown to you, will distress you. But if you ask about them while the Qur'an is being revealed, they will be shown to you." (TMQ 5:101). The revelation and religion being complete and perfected, the prescribed elements of religion are known, permitting no addition, and the forbidden elements of worldly existence are likewise known, making permissible all which has not been forbidden. Discussion and picky investigation into that which Allah chose not to pass ruling upon should be abstained from.
[10] Daraqutni (42, 104)

In addition, Allah Most High conveyed,

1. "And whatever the Messenger☙has given you, take; and what he has forbidden you, refrain from. And fear Allah; indeed, Allah is severe in penalty." (TMQ 59:7)
2. "Those who follow the messenger [i.e., Muhammad☙], the unlettered prophet whom they find written [i.e., mentioned] in what they have of the Torah and the Gospel, who enjoins upon them what is right and forbids them what is wrong and makes lawful for them the good things and prohibits from them the evil..." (TMQ 7:157)
3. "It is He who created for you all of that which is on the earth." (TMQ 2:29 – which implies the permissibility of all that which is not forbidden of worldly matters.)
4. "Say, 'Who has forbidden the adornment of [i.e., from] Allah which He has produced for His servants and the good [lawful] things of provision?" (TMQ 7:32 – which indicates the error in forbidding that which Allah Most High has *not* forbidden of worldly matters.)

So this general principle of everything of worship being forbidden except that which is prescribed, and everything of worldly matters being permitted except that which has been forbidden, is not only well supported, but of potent impact. As it relates to the subject under discussion, those who seek an easier path in terms of physical existence and worldly matters are encouraged to do so, for an authentic hadith relates that "The prophet☙was never given a choice between two things except that he chose the easier one as long as it was not a sin."[11] However, those who seek innovation in matters of worship are to be censured and/or condemned. Imam Malik commented,

> "He who innovates something for the *ummah* today which the pious predecessors were not upon, then he has proclaimed that the prophet (i.e., Muhammad☙) had betrayed the *ummah*, because Allah the Almighty has said, 'Today I have completed your religion.' That which was not part of the religion at that time (i.e., of Muhammad☙ and of his companions) is not part of the religion today."[12]

The point is that while the possibilities for improvement of the human condition in worldly terms are vast, there is a bare minimum in terms of beliefs and practices which, if transgressed, compromises a person's claim to the religion. The minimum requirements of Islamic faith are clearly defined, one example of which is to be found in the following hadith:

> A man from Najd with unkempt hair came to Allah's Messenger☙and we heard his loud voice but could not understand what he was saying, till he came near (and then we came to know) that he was asking about Islam. Allah's Messenger☙said, "You have to perform five *Salat* (prayers) in a day and night (24 hours)." The man asked, "Are there any other (more) *Salat* (prayers) upon me?" Allah's Messenger☙

---

[11] Bukhari (3367), Muslim (2327), Muwatta Imam Malik (1603)
[12] Al-Ih'kam, by Ibn Hazim

replied, "No, but if you want to perform the *Nawafil* (i.e., supererogatory, or nonobligatory) *Salat* (you can)." Allah's Messenger ﷺ further said to him: "You have to observe *Saum* [fasts (according to Islamic teachings)] during the month of Ramadan." The man asked, "Are there any other (more) fasting upon me?" Allah's Messenger ﷺ replied, "No, but if you want to observe the *Nawafil* fasts (you can)." Then Allah's Messenger ﷺ further said to him, "You have to pay the *Zakat*." The man asked, "Is there any thing other than the *Zakat* for me to pay?" Allah's Messenger ﷺ replied, "No, unless you want to give alms of your own." And then that man retreated saying, "By Allah! I will neither do less nor more than this." Allah's Messenger ﷺ said, "If he is true to his word, then he will be successful (i.e., he will be granted Paradise)"[13]

This hadith effectively sums up the minimum limits of Islamic practice, while at the same time concluding that satisfying these minimum limits leads to the reward of paradise.

This formula does, of course, make sense, for mankind lives such formulas every day in a thousand ways. For example, the body requires a minimum amount of oxygen to survive, and a minimum core body temperature. Maintain those minimums, and a person survives. Transgress those minimums by the smallest degree, and death results. Similarly, a car requires a minimum amount of gas to get from one point to another. Even one drop less than the bare minimum means the car stops short – albeit by only a drop's worth of distance. But short nonetheless. Sure, a person could say, "Heck, just park the car and walk it." But there are some things a person simply cannot walk off. Failure is one of them. One point less than an 'A' on the exam is no longer an 'A.' One gram less than an ounce is no longer an ounce. One step behind the winner is second place. One second too long underwater is drowning. And one drop less than the required minimum means drawing up short.

Maintain a higher oxygenation and body temperature than the required minimum, and a person will not only feel better, but be at less risk of disaster. Keep more gas in the car than required, and a person will have a greater reserve, just in case. A person *can* live the bare minimums -- life on the edge, so to speak -- but this is risky, uncomfortable and, under normal circumstances, unnecessarily foolish. Far better to live well within the critical limits. So too, with religion. People who live the bare minimums of faith and practice teeter on the fence of their faith, every day risking the consequences of falling to the wrong side. On the other hand, those who perfect their faith, practice, and worship live within the expanded safety zones encountered at the higher levels of religiosity.

So while living life on the edge has become trendy in the arenas of extreme sports and high finance, where a person can achieve fame or fortune at the risk of personal injury or bankruptcy, living religion on the edge risks a person's salvation for…well, for what, exactly? A few more minutes saved from prayer, a few more mouthfuls saved from fasting, a few more dollars saved from charity? A small price for salvation, a person would think, and definitely worth sacrificing for the benefit of expanded safety

---

[13] Bukhari (42) and Muslim (11)

and comfort zones. And it is not as if a person need compromise all other elements of worldly existence.

On the contrary, Muslims live remarkably clean, honest, wholesome and satisfying lives. And in tribute to the success of the Islamic standard, the fields of politics, personal conduct, family and social structure, economics, civil and criminal law, and many other disciplines of human existence in the Islamic world have enjoyed some of the greatest duration and success due to the sound religious principles upon which they were founded. The Islamic religion itself is practiced today as it was in the time of the prophet, Muhammad 鷺, making Islam the only Abrahamic religion practiced today in the purity of the original. If ever there was a success record that bears witness to the truth, that is it. Furthermore, Allah conveyed the promise that there will always be a group of people on the right, for authentic hadith relates Muhammad 鷺 as having taught, "There will always be a group of my *ummah* (i.e., nation) openly on the truth until the Day of Judgment."[14]

Let's try to be amongst them.

---

[14]Bukhari (3441), Muslim (156), Abu Dawud (4252), Tirmidhi (2229)

16

2) The Pillars

Once a person enters Islam, the question becomes, "What do I do now?" The short answer is, "Go home, take a shower, and start praying."

Upon entering Islam, it is preferred for a person to perform a purification ritual, which consists of bathing the entire body in water. This ritual is usually private, and like baptism is symbolic of rebirth in a newness of spirit. The Islamic religion teaches that when a person becomes Muslim, all his or her prior sins are forgiven. Just as the soul is cleansed of sins by the pure truth of the testimony of faith, the body is cleansed symbolically with the purity of water.

The physical practices that become incumbent upon the convert are five, the first being to make *shahada* (testimony of faith), understanding that along with the *shahada* a person also implicitly acknowledges the fundamentals of faith (belief in Allah, His angels, the revealed scriptures, the messengers, the Hereafter, and Divine decree). The four subsequent required duties consist of prayer five times daily (at prescribed intervals, and in accordance with Islamic rules of prayer and purification), annual fasting of the month of Ramadan, annual payment of the *zakat* (poor-due), and pilgrimage to Mecca during the period of *Haj*, once in a lifetime, if physically and financially capable. Now, remembering the lesson from above, the first question should not be, "Well, okay, but how do I do those things?" Rather, the first question should be, "Okay, fine, but please, first tell me where you get this teaching."

Answer: Qur'an and Sunnah. With regard to the fundamentals of faith, TMQ 2:177 includes the following: "...(true) righteousness is (in) one who believes in Allah, the Last Day, the angels, the Book, and the prophets..." With regard to the five pillars of Islam, "...(true) righteousness is (in) one who...establishes prayer and gives *zakah*..." (TMQ 2:177), "O you who have believed, decreed upon you is fasting..." (TMQ 2:183-185), and "And complete the haj and 'umrah for Allah." (TMQ 2:196) In multiple passages in the Holy Qur'an these beliefs are restated, reemphasized and/or clarified, either together or separately, and the oneness, omnipotence and Divine decree of Allah is stressed over and again. The above are just a small taste of the supportive teachings from the Qur'an. From the Sunnah we find what has come to be known as the Gabriel hadith, related by Umar (companion of Muhammadﷺ, and second Caliph):

> "One day while we were sitting with the messenger of Allahﷺ there came before us a man with extremely white clothing and extremely black hair. There were no signs of travel on him and none of us knew him. He [came and] sat next to the Prophetﷺ. He supported his knees up against the knees of the Prophetﷺ and put his hands on his thighs. He said, "O Muhammadﷺ, tell me about Islam." The Messenger of Allahﷺ said, "Islam is to testify that there is none worthy of worship except Allah and that Muhammadﷺ is the Messenger of Allah, to establish the prayers, to pay the zakat, to fast [the month of] Ramadhaan, and to make the pilgrimage to the House if you have the means to do so." He said, "You have spoken truthfully [or correctly]." We were amazed that he asks the question and then he says that he had spoken truthfully. He said, "Tell me about *Imaan* (faith)." He [the

Messenger of Allahﷺ]responded, "It is to believe in Allah, His angels, His books, His messengers, the Last Day and to believe in divine decree, [both] the good and the evil thereof." He said, "Tell me about al-Ihsaan (god-consciousness)." He [the Prophetﷺ] answered, "It is that you worship Allah as if you see Him, and even though you do not see Him, [you know] He sees you." He said, "Tell me about [the time of] the Hour." He [the Prophetﷺ] answered, "The one being asked does not know more than the one asking." He said, "Tell me about its signs." He answered, "The slave-girl shall give birth to her mistress, and you will see the barefooted, scantily-clothed, destitute shepherds competing in constructing lofty buildings." Then he went away. I stayed for a long time. Then he [the Prophetﷺ]said, "O Umar, do you know who the questioner was?" I said, "Allah and His Messengerﷺ know best." He said: "It was [the angel] Gabriel, who came to you to teach you your religion."[15]

And,

> Islam has been built on five (pillars): testifying that there is no deity but Allah and that Muhammadﷺ is the messenger of Allah, establishing the prayers, paying the *zakat*, making the pilgrimage to the House, and fasting in Ramadan."[16]

So, having established the authority of the teachings, we can continue.

The rituals of prayer take time to learn, and a convert comes to understand that Allah excuses shortcomings in the beginning, so long as converts make their effort to learn and improve. Nonetheless, the prayers need to be made in their time, and the duty is upon the convert to learn and perfect the prayer as quickly as possible, and in accordance with the manner and conditions of prayer according to the *Shari'a*.

At some point in the first year, the Muslim convert will encounter the fast of the month of Ramadan, and the season of *haj* (pilgrimage) to Mecca, which follows the fast of Ramadan by two lunar months. Both of these two pillars demonstrate the practicality of the Islamic religion, for although fasting for the first time can be a formidable experience for some, the convert can take comfort in knowing that an inability to fast can be compensated. And for that matter, fasting is not required for those who find themselves unable due to hardship such as poor health or advanced age. Similarly, *haj* is a duty upon those Muslims who have the ability (both physical and financial), but those who do not have the ability are excused for as long as their circumstances constrain them. However, the importance of these religious pillars should not be underestimated, and a person should only accept dispensation if truly unable to perform the required ritual. For example, Umar (companion to Muhammadﷺ and the second Caliph) stressed the importance of the *haj* by teaching that "the Muslim who has the ability to perform *haj* but doesn't do it, and who dies in that state, then let him die as a Jew or as a Christian."[17]

---

[15] Muslim (8)
[16] Bukhari (8), Muslim (16)
[17] Bayhaqi (8444)

18

Payment of *zakat*, the poor-due, is the last of the five pillars of Islam to become due upon the convert, for the *zakat* is paid once a year. Perhaps one of the most poorly understood of the pillars of practice, *zakat* is not a tithe, for *zakat* is not a percentage of income. Some people need their entire income to live, and as such, cannot afford to pay anything. *Zakat*, then, is not a percentage of income, but rather a percentage of *excess* wealth, meaning that Muslims are commanded to pay a small (either 2.5% or 5%, depending on category) poor-due on wealth possessed above and beyond needs for a period of one year. Hence, if a person has a million dollars for eleven months, but loses it in the twelfth, no *zakat* is owed. Likewise, if a person starts the year with a house, a car, and a salary, even a high salary at that, but ends the year with the same house, car, and salary, but nothing saved in excess of needs for the preceding year, no *zakat* is due. *Zakat* is only due on those elements of wealth (ex: money, gold, crops, goods of merchandise intended for sale, livestock, etc.), in excess of a person's needs, which a person possesses for a complete year. [18]

The above discussion provides only the briefest introduction, for each of the five pillars of Islam can be discussed in a book devoted solely to the subject, and in fact, all have. Many times over, for that matter. And once again, the point of this present book is not to duplicate the information that is already available, but rather to suggest the best way in which converts to Islam can integrate the practices of the religion into their lives. With respect to the present subject, the easiest thing would be to recommend one or a number of books on the subject of the pillars of Islam, and then move on to the next topic. But not so fast. There is a difficulty here that quickly becomes apparent, and which must be resolved before moving on.

And this is important, if not key. The issue is this: given the clear and simple foundation of Islam, being the revealed word of Allah in the Holy Qur'an and the example of the messenger, Muhammad ﷺ, as recorded in the Sunnah (hadith), a person might expect one distinct and authoritative answer to any one simple and straight-forward question. And, 80-90% of the time, that fair expectation is satisfied. But not always. 10-20% of religious issues do not achieve unanimous scholarly agreement. Now, some find that lack of scholarly consensus disturbing, but in fact, it is to be tolerated and respected. Let me explain.

---

[18] Islamically speaking, a certain amount of monetary wealth is *zakat*-exempt. The zakat-exempt amount is equivalent to the market value of 85 grams of gold or 595 grams of silver, whichever is less. Zakat is due on monetary wealth in excess of this amount, if possessed for one full year.

2.a.) Differences

As a new Muslim, I pondered this issue of scholarly disagreement with a certain confusion. For roughly two years I struggled with this issue until one day I met a Moroccan brother on the streets of Cambridge, England, while walking to the Friday congregational prayer (*Salat aj-Jum'ah*). We fell into discussion of this point, whereupon he pointed to a building and said words to the effect of, "You see this building? Well, I'm a structural engineer. And I can tell you that all buildings are designed to have a certain degree of flexibility. This is necessary, for all buildings must be able to flex with the wind, with tremors or earthquakes, even with temperature changes. If a building is too rigid it will prove brittle, and the least little stress will lead to fractures, structural disruption, and eventual collapse. The same is true with religion. There has to be flexibility in a religion, and in Islam that flexibility is to be found in scholarly differences."

To a large degree, this brother helped me to begin to comprehend the divine wisdom behind this issue. With time, I came to understand several points, the first being that the scholars of Islam do agree on all of the important issues – it is only the small, subsidiary issues upon which there is disagreement. For example, the scholars agree on the requirement of five daily prayers and the conditions of prayer, such as ritual purity of person, place, and clothing, most of the integrals of the prayer itself and the conditions that validate and invalidate the prayer, etc. However, scholarly disagreement does exist over some small, subsidiary issues, such as where Muslims should hold their hands while standing during prayer, how they should point their finger during sitting, whether the *Basmallah* (the first line of Al-Fatiha, most commonly translated to the meaning "In the name of Allah, the Most Gracious, the Most Merciful") should be recited silently or out loud, etc. These differences in opinion are to be accepted and tolerated, for the great scholars of the past were unable to resolve these differences, despite a level of knowledge and wisdom that eclipses that of the scholars of the present.

And while it is true that certain issues benefit from further inspection, the fact of the matter is that the main momentum of *fiqh* in the present age is directed to legal rulings on new issues brought on by social, political, and technological change. Attempts at rectifying thousand year old disagreements are few, and typically prove fruitless and frustrating. Furthermore, such efforts frequently divide Muslims into separate camps at odds with one another over petty and, in the big scheme of things, relatively insignificant issues. And one thing Muslims do not need is more causes of division.

It is a sad fact that Muslims frequently focus their attention more on the few small details over which they differ than on the vast foundation of the religion upon which they agree – in other words, the really important issues of life and religion. It is a disturbing truth that during periods when Muslims were being starved, raped, tortured, and/or slaughtered in Palestine, Bosnia, Afghanistan, Chechnya, Kashmir, Burma, etc., Muslims in American and England were arguing about whether they should line up for prayer by the tips of their toes, by the ankles, or by the heels of their feet.

Perhaps this focusing upon smaller issues is just part of the pickiness of human nature, but then again, perhaps it is a tool of the *Shaitan* (Satan) to distract the Muslims from the more critical issues of their lives and religion. Whichever is the case, the effect is destructive and, to the sincere convert, disturbing. On one hand, the convert embraces Islam seeking a world of spiritual peace through religious certainty. On the other hand, the convert finds the Muslims arguing, and sometimes even fighting, over picky little differences that are best tolerated and left alone, rather than celebrating solidarity of true faith.

Having said all that, a person naturally assumes there to be only one correct answer to any one question, and desires to rectify any differences that *do* exist. Sometimes this is possible, and sometimes not, but 100% of the time it is simply not necessary, for the essentials of the Islamic religion are clear and agreed upon by *ijma* (consensus) of the Sunni scholars, and disagreement over the small subsidiary elements is easily excused on the basis of the Islamic teaching that actions are judged by intention (authentic hadith relates that the prophet taught, "Actions are by intention, and every person will receive what he intended."[19]), in combination with the relative insignificance of such differences.

The point is that the process of resolving Islamic issues does not always result in correctness or uniformity of judgment, and this is okay. Nobody is perfect and even scholars are subject to differences in opinion and even error at times. Mistakes may be made, but in the Islamic religion the qualifications of the person making the mistake comes into consideration. Mistakes made by scholars stand to be excused by Allah Most High, whereas mistakes in legal judgment made by laity stand to be punished. For the question is not limited to whether a specific legal judgment is right or wrong, but also involves whether the *process* of making that judgment is correct. Scholars are obligated by their gift of knowledge to pass judgment according to their level of expertise, and all others are obligated to follow. Laity, however, become blameworthy if they pass judgment inappropriate for their level of training and knowledge. Westerners, typically raised to question authority at every level, may find this formula vexing or uncomfortable, but nonetheless, that is the Islamic tradition with regard to scholarship.

The above does not imply that a person can not, or should not, question the evidence to support any scholar's particular judgment. No…such questions are usually well received, so long as the student asks in the process of seeking knowledge, and not in an attempt to challenge or disprove the scholar -- such argumentative behavior can be acceptable from others of similar scholastic standing, but is generally regarded as inappropriate or disrespectful on the part of a student. So questioning authority is acceptable if done with humility and good manners for, as stated above, actions are judged by intentions.

With time and education, the new Muslim typically comes to appreciate the extraordinarily strict standards of qualified Islamic scholarship, which prove daunting to those raised in an educational institute of the relatively soft academic standards of Western scholarship.[20] Once a convert or student of the religion comes to recognize

---

[19] Bukhari (1), Muslim (1907)

[20] For explanation of the qualifications of Islamic scholarship, see

    1) *Principles of Islamic Jurisprudence*, by Mohammad Hashim Kamali, Islamic Texts Society, pp. 374-379 (chapter entitled: Conditions [Shurut] of Ijtihad).

the vast difference between scholars and laity in Islam, the need to submit to the greater qualifications of the scholars becomes apparent. Furthermore, the peace, safety, and ease of adopting such a practice is no stranger to converts to the religion, many of whom struggle to rediscover the feeling of peace that initially accompanies conversion to Islam. The peace of living a life and religion of truth, the safety of following the decisions of the scholars, and the ease of implementing the religion based on qualified scholarship is readily apparent to all who have embraced the simplicity of such a path. In such a design the scholars bear the responsibility of their decisions, the students and laity bear the responsibility of adhering to the teachings of the scholars, and everyone goes home happy, fulfilled, and at ease due to being procedurally correct. On the other hand, those inclined to attempting to reinvent the wheel of *fiqh* typically find themselves given over to argument and discord, with the peace and ease of the correct and safest path disrupted by the futile effort of redefining *fiqh* from a foundation of immature, unqualified scholarship.

But what if a mistake *is* made? This question haunts the hearts and minds of the believer, for true believers frequently struggle over issues of minor importance out of zeal for perfection of faith and worship. But the point is this: if everybody is doing what they should be doing, nobody is blameworthy. Islam teaches that Allah assigns a scholar the reward of one good deed for exerting him- or herself in arriving at a judgment, and the reward of another good deed for being correct. Hence, scholars are rewarded with two good deeds if correct in judgment, and one good deed if incorrect, simply for having fulfilled the responsibility of asserting the knowledge with which they were entrusted. Laity have a different level of responsibility, and are rewarded for the fulfillment of their duty of following the scholars. In return, laity are not to be held accountable for adhering to unclear errors on the part of scholars, for laity are not expected to have the scholastic tools to be able to know better. So if scholars determine *fiqh* according to their abilities (without shirking their duties and without overstepping the limits of their scholarship), and if laity follow the *fiqh* laid down by respected scholars (following the opinion of those scholars whom they judge most knowledgeable and trustworthy, and not making a mockery of the process by seeking the opinion they desire, wherever they can find it), then everybody would be correct in process, nobody would be blameworthy, and all can be relaxed, happy, and at peace with both their family in faith and Allah.

---

2) *Studies in Usul Ul Fiqh*, by Iyad Hilal, (Islamic Cultural Workshop, P.O. Box 1932, Walnut, CA 91789, (909) 399-4708), Section 8.1 – Qualifications for Performing Ijtihad, pp 103-105.

The above two books define the qualifications of a *mujtahid* (an Islamic scholar qualified to derive *fiqh*). In order to begin to understand the complexities of the list of qualifications discussed, the reader is further referred to:

1) *An Introduction to the Sciences of the Qur'aan*, by Abu Ammaar Yasir Qadhi, Al-Hidaayah Publishing.
2) *Studies in Hadith Methodology and Literature*, by Muhammad Mustafa Azami, American Trust Publications.
3) *Hadith Literature: Its Origins, Development and Special Features*, by Muhammad Zubayr Siddiqi, Islamic Texts Society.

Note: The reader need not study the above books in depth, but should at least delve into the contents to the point that the mind begins to wander, swimming in the swirl of complexities, for it is at this point that modesty should prevail, with the hoped-for result of dampening inclination to personal judgment in matters of *fiqh*, combined with appreciation of the rare genius of those individuals to have achieved the status of mujtahid.

So why doesn't it work out that way?

Simply because there is so much religious over-zeal, disagreement and intolerance when it comes to differences in *fiqh*. Being rigid and uncompromising may be good when it comes to issues of *aqeeda* (creed), which permit little or no room for variance, but scholastic differences in *fiqh* have been recognized, tolerated, and respected since the time of the early scholars. Those Muslims who are disrespectful of these differences fight an uphill battle against an avalanche of over a thousand years of peaceful scholarly coexistence, despite *fiqh* differences that defy resolution. Such Muslims are typically disruptive, loud, intolerant, rigid and uncompromising, and are frequently found in the center of any argument, expressing the strongest of opinions with the loudest of voices, least knowledge and minimal manners. Unfortunately, they are so common in the Americas, England, and Western Europe as to exert a presence in virtually every Mosque in the Western world. Such individuals are to be wary of, counseled and, if need be, avoided. Sometimes they calm down and mellow with time, sometimes not. It is an uphill battle that is frequently frustrating and often lost. But perhaps such individuals will listen to the best of advice, for in the Holy Qur'an the righteous servant, Luqman, is recorded as having counseled his son to the effect,

> "O my son, establish prayer, enjoin what is right, forbid what is wrong, and be patient over what befalls you. Indeed, [all] that is of the matters [requiring] determination. And do not turn your cheek [in contempt] toward people and do not walk through the earth exultantly. Indeed, Allah does not like everyone self-deluded and boastful. And be moderate in your pace and lower your voice; indeed, the most disagreeable of sounds is the voice of donkeys." (TMQ 31:17-19)

Furthermore, one of the struggles of the convert is to maintain a sense of inner peace, which can be difficult when conflicting scholarly opinions distract from learning the essentials of faith and practice. However, I would offer the advice that Islam is the religion of the middle path, and when a person searches with sincerity, that middle path can almost always be found. The middle path is a path of moderation, about which previous generations coined the teaching, "moderation in all things." As relates to the practice of Islam, a better Western proverb may be hard to find. Should convert Muslims seek to live the straight, middle path of Islam, I would simply advise them to seek out the quiet, unobtrusive Muslims who seem to be practicing their religion with graceful avoidance of the loud, disruptive members of the Muslim community. A person can't go far wrong remembering the opening words of *Desiderada*:

> "Go placidly amid the noise and the haste,
> and remember what peace there may be in silence.
> As far as possible, without surrender,
> be on good terms with all persons.
> Speak your truth quietly and clearly;
> and listen to others, even the dull and ignorant;
> They too have their story.
> Avoid loud and aggressive persons;
> They are vexatious to the spirit..."

The scholars, on the other hand, nurture and warm the spirit. They are to be found in the circles of knowledge, good manners, and good will. Peace and security is to be found in their company and teachings.

2.b.) Scholars, and Fiqh (Islamic Law)

As discussed above, all groups that claim the banner of Islam, whether correct, deviant, or even completely out of Islam, profess to follow the Qur'an and Sunnah, as interpreted by 'the scholars' (or *'ulema'* in Arabic). *'Ulema'* sounds so exotic and authoritative that a person can easily be seduced by the comment that, "The *ulema* of Islam teach..." or "The *ulema* of Islam say..." But who are this elusive *'ulema'* that everybody claims to be following? Quite obviously, various groups have equally various opinions on which body of scholars or pseudo-scholars constitute their concept of *THE 'ulema.'* How, then, does a convert to the religion know who the true scholars are, and make sense of the issues upon which they differ?

To begin with, a person has to understand that scholarly differences regarding the subsidiary elements of Islamic *fiqh* is to be respected and tolerated. On the other hand, issues that have achieved *ijma* (consensus) of the scholars are to be upheld and *not* debated. Hence, there may be room for polite investigation and debate, *amongst the students of knowledge and scholars*, on issues of scholastic difference, but there is little or no room for debate on issues that have achieved *ijma* of the scholars, whether among the Imams of the four Madhhabs (school of legal thought)[21] or among the respected scholars of later periods in Islamic history. Furthermore, those who debate issues of *fiqh* without sufficient knowledge or training are to be avoided at all cost, for this is the territory of qualified scholars, and qualified scholars only. TMQ 4:83 relates,

> "And when there comes to them something (i.e., information) about [public] security or fear, they spread it around. But if they had referred it back to the Messenger 鏐 or to those of authority among them, then the ones who [can] draw correct conclusions from it would have known about it. And if not for the favor of Allah upon you and His mercy, you would have followed Satan, except for a few."

So to begin with, Muslims should stop risking their salvation on the opinions of unqualified Muslims whose misguidance can approximate that of the *Shaitan* (Satan). Secondly, they should stop fighting over the small, subsidiary issues upon which 1,400 years of valid scholarship has not agreed, and which are not terribly important in any case. For example, issues of *aqeeda* (creed) are of far greater importance than where people place their feet and hands during prayer. Similarly, Muslims need to stop challenging the issues, both large and small, upon which 1,400 years of scholarship has unanimously agreed, for unless one is of scholastic standing to rival the great scholars of the past, these issues are decided and dead.

Next, Muslims should recognize that there are practical aspects to approaching Islamic knowledge. The new convert needs to be directed to the correct path as early as possible, made comfortable thereupon, and most importantly, not blown out of the religion by incessant and insistent disagreement. Religious over-steering is a common syndrome for the new convert, brought on by the confusion of encountering multiple

---

[21] Most Muslims in the world follow one of the four Madhhabs (These are known as the Shafi, Hanafi, Hambali, and Maliki Madhhabs, after the names of the Imams whose interpretations of the Islamic evidences formed the foundation of each Madhhab).

strong and conflicting viewpoints. Radical shifts from one extreme of thought to another, frequently crossing the straight and middle path of moderation with wide, sinusoidal swings out of control and largely devoid of direction, is scary and confusing, and not just to the convert. While new converts may initially suffer confusion and insecurity from failing to find comfortable and definitive guidance, those close to them, namely concerned friends and family whom the new Muslim hopes to reach with Islamic *dawa* (invitation), may be negatively impacted by witnessing the wild and indecisive swings in thought and practice typical of the Western convert. The new convert may eventually get a handle on the religion and dampen the swings, but many do not and some, worn down by an inability to steer straight, so to speak, leave Islam entirely.

Aqeeda is usually not the main issue of confusion for the new convert, for correctness of *aqeeda* is usually the reason for conversion in the first place. Most new converts enter Islam as a result of having found the simple Qur'anic teachings of *aqeeda* and *tawheed* to match their inborn template of belief. Only later do *aqeeda* differences sometimes become an item of study, as discussed below.

Differences in *fiqh*, however, usually *are* the main issue of confusion. The new convert frequently has the experience of going to pray for the first time and being told to line up by the toes, place your hands like this, do such-and-such with your finger while sitting, sit in such-and-such a manner, etc. The next day, some well-meaning brother or sister may observe the new convert and feel compelled to instruct lining up by the heels or ankles, holding the hands elsewhere, wiggling the finger instead of pointing, etc. After a few rounds of well-intentioned brothers or sisters bouncing the new convert off the various walls of minor but conflicting *fiqh*, some converts get fed up and give up, leaving the well-intentioned but disorienting brothers and sisters to wonder what they did wrong, when in fact they had simply confused the convert out of the mosque with an overload of conflicting information.

So what is the safest and best path by which new Muslims may learn and practice their religion of Islam? The answer to that question varies from one 'scholar' to another, but thankfully offers only a few possibilities. To begin with, many scholars and imams tend to recommend more modern books of Islamic jurisprudence, such as *Fiqh us-Sunnah*, by Sayyid Saabiq, smaller treatises by Nasr Ad-Deen Al-Albaani and others, and self-study of collections of hadith and *tafseer*. Others direct the new Muslim to fundamental books of one of the four Madhhabs. *Al-Nawawi's Manual of Islam* and *Reliance of the Traveler*, both translated by Nuh Ha Mim Keller, are the best translations of foundational books of Shafi *fiqh* into the English language known to *this* author, although they both bear the unfortunate taint of the translator's strong dedication to Sufism and Ashari *aqeeda*.

That said, all of the above books have their proponents and antagonists, and each individual simply has to investigate the various opinions in order to decide which to follow. Initially, that is. Not surprisingly, many who at first embark upon one path of study eventually gravitate towards another. This process is not altogether unhealthy, for people can best choose their direction after weighing all the options. I would suggest, however, that much of the initial indecision and vacillation between schools of thought results from misunderstanding the roles of the Madhhabs and what is known, in present day terms, as the Salafi movement. Many conceive these two entities to be in conflict with one another, and outwardly this may appear to be true. However, when investigated, Muslims usually come to appreciate that these two schools of thought are, in fact, complementary, for the Madhhabs were originally developed as schools of *fiqh*, whereas the Salafi movement is one of Islamic reform. The Salafi reforms primarily focus upon correcting those errors which had grown to corrupt the Muslim *ummah* in general and the Madhhab system in specific, with the major issues being:

1) Errors in *aqeeda*, which became institutionalized in the Madhhabs through the regrettable adoption of the Ashari and Maturidi *aqeedas*;

2) The practice of Sufism, which not only became fanatical and extreme, but which also became seemingly inextricably bonded with the Madhhabs following the period of Abu Haamid Muhammad al-Ghazali (1058-1111 C.E.);

3) The relative unwillingness of Madhhab scholars to modify the *fiqh* of their Madhhab when presented with conflicting hadith evidence, despite the religious mandate to do so when encountering valid hadith evidence;[22]

4) *Taqleed*, or blind following, on the part of the Madhhab adherents;

5) And the infiltration of non-religious customs (including those revived from the period of ignorance) into the practices of the Islamic religion.

The Salafi movement is not, and never has been, primarily a *fiqh* movement, and the Madhhabs are practically nothing but. So, in fact, these two schools support and complement one another. The *fiqh* of the Madhhabs forms the foundation upon which modern *fiqh* research is largely based, whereas Salafi ideology identifies and corrects those errors which, over the centuries, surreptitiously crept into the beliefs and practices of the Muslims, most of whom adhered to one of the four Madhhabs. So complete and universal was the infiltration of Sufism and either Ashari or Maturidi

---

[22] The four Madhhabs claim a dynamic structure with the provision for progressive *fiqh* modification given new knowledge. However, such changes are in scarce evidence, and a person is hard put to find changes in mainstream Madhhab *fiqh* given what many have argued to be relatively conclusive evidence. The following statements by the imams of the four Madhhabs apply:

1. Abu Hanifah – "When the Hadith is authentic, then. that is my Madhhab" (Ibn Abidin, *Al Hashiyah*, p. 1/63) and "If I make a statement at variance with that which is in the book of Allah, or at variance with the statement of His Messenger, then leave my statement." (Al-Fulani, *I'qath Al Himam*, p. 50)

2. Malik – "I am only a man; I make mistakes and am at times correct. Therefore look at my opinions; everything that agrees with the book and the Sunnah then take it, and everything that does not agree with them then leave it. (Ibn Abd Al Barr, *Al Jami*, p. 2/32)

3. Shafi – "When the Hadith is authentic, then that is my Madhhab" (Al-Nawawi, *Al Majmu*, p. 1/136); "Every issue in which there is an authentic statement narrated from the Messenger of Allah and it goes against that which I have said, then I go back on my statement during my life and after it" (Abu Nafiim, *Al Hilyah*, p. 9/107); and "Every hadith from the Prophet, then take it as my opinion, even if you did not hear it from me (Ibn Abi Hatim, *Adab Al Shafi*, pp. 93-94); "There is consensus amongst the Muslims that he who is shown the Sunnah of the Prophet is forbidden to leave it for the saying of anyone, no matter who that person may be (Al Fulani, *I'qath Al Himam*, p. 68)

4. Ahmad ibn Hanbal – "Do not blindly follow me, nor Malik, nor Shafi, nor Al-Awzafii, nor Al-Thawri. Instead, take from where they took" (Al Fulani, *I'qath Al Himam*, p. 113).

aqeeda into the Madhhab world that, in time, they came to be considered integral with the Madhhabs. Such does not reflect the thinking at the period of origins, and the Muslim world has the Salafi's to thank for identifying and announcing that fact.

Having said that, a person can easily understand why the Salafi movement and the Madhhabs are frequently considered at odds with one another. For although in truth they are not, in practice the adherents to these different schools frequently fail to separate the issues. Too many ignorant 'Salafi's' reflexively dismiss the *fiqh* of the Madhhabs, throwing the baby out with the bathwater, so to speak, because they do not differentiate between the importance of the *fiqh* of the Madhhabs and the deviations in belief and practice which became associated with Madhhabs over time. Other Salafi's erroneously consider differences in *fiqh* to be the main issue, whereas in fact the main issues are those listed above. On the other side of the equation, Madhhab adherents frequently view Salafi's with animosity because Salafi ideology challenges the *aqeeda* and Sufism which they have come to consider integral with their particular Madhhab. This animosity is, of course, real, and upon these issues a person simply has to take sides -- for or against Sufism, for or against Ashari or Maturidi *aqeeda*, etc. Let us recognize, however, that it is not the *fiqh* of the Madhhabs that is being challenged so much as the errors in *aqeeda*, deviation into Sufism, stagnation in *fiqh*, blind following on the part of the adherents, and adoption of non-Islamic practices.

The end result is that those Muslims with balance typically align themselves upon a middle path between extremes, seeking the good within both groups, which in the opinion of this author means recognizing the excellence of the *fiqh* of the Madhhabs on one hand, and the merit of Salafi reforms on the other.

This opinion is not without precedent, for all of the scholars who revived Salafi ideology (including Shaykh al-Islam Ibn Taymeeyah, Ibn Qayyim al-Jawzeeyah, and Muhammad ibn Abdul-Wahhaab), began their studies as adherents to one of the traditional Madhhabs, endorsed this pathway of study, and never sought to overthrow any of these schools of *fiqh*. Rather, they sought to revive the Madhhabs, but at the same time reform the manner in which were followed. Furthermore, none of these scholars ever claimed to have established a new school of *fiqh*, despite the fact that, given their popularity and scholastic achievement, they undoubtedly could have had they thought it appropriate. And, in fact, at each point of history during the past millennia the vast majority of Muslims, laity and scholars alike (Salafi scholars included), have adhered to one of the four traditional Madhhabs.

In light of the above, and considering that the majority of Muslims have been united upon the process of following the *fiqh* of the Madhhabs for over a thousand years, a person might wish to recall the hadith that records Muhammad ﷺ as having taught, "My *ummah* (nation) will never unite upon an error."[23]

Some scholars (typically those of the Madhhabs) consider the following of a Madhhab to be obligatory upon laity, whereas others (typically those of the Salafi movement) do not. Whichever opinion a person accepts, it would be good to notice that virtually all scholars, regardless of school, recognize and honor the excellence of the *fiqh* of the four Madhhabs.

---

[23] Tirmidhi (2167), Ibn Majah (3950), Ahmad (17060)

Similarly, the merits of the Salafi movement are numerous, and relatively transparent. To begin with, if the Salafi pathway is defined as the pathway of emulating the righteous predecessors and the best of this *ummah* of Islam, which is to say, the companions of Muhammadﷺ (i.e., the *salaf,* from which the movement gets its name), then should not all Muslims aspire to this accomplishment? For which Muslim would not like to be like the *salaf?* Secondly, if the Salafi movement is defined as a movement to correct the deviations listed above, should not all Muslims aspire to membership? The problem, then, is simply that with regard to *fiqh* there is no agreed upon body of teachings defined as the *fiqh* of the Salafi movement. Rather, there are many books and treatises, some as short as pamphlets, others in voluminous tomes (such as the teachings and *fatwas* of Shaykh al-Islam Ibn Taymeeyah), which complement the body of *fiqh* literature. And because many of these books and treatises are translated into the English language they are readily available, of practical size, and highly useful. To argue that these books replace the *fiqh* of the four Madhhabs, however, is a precarious position, and the cause of much discord and division amongst those who argue such issues.

Both the Madhhab and Salafi groups, then, have great practicality once their strengths and limitations are recognized. Of course, there are those on the edges of extremes who categorically condemn any school other than their own, but more moderate Muslims seek a middle path between the limits of these extremes, and recognize the good of both the *fiqh* of the Madhhabs and the reforms of the Salafi movement. And this is exactly what many Salafi scholars have done, by following Salafi teachings with regard to *aqeeda* and purification of the soul (which equates to rejection of the derived teachings of the Ashari and Maturidi schools, with regard to *aqeeda,* and of Sufism, with regard to spiritual purification, in favor of the clear teachings of the Qur'an, Sunnah, and first three generations of pious Muslims), and a specific Madhhab with regard to *fiqh* (but remaining mindful of the mandate to assign priority to the Islamic evidences over the teachings of any specific Maddhab, when the two are in conflict, and by this means avoiding the error of blind following).

Returning to the subject of *fiqh* books, *Fiqh as-Sunnah,* by Sayyid Saabiq, is widely respected (especially in Egypt) and is a frequent starting place for many new converts. *Fiqh as-Sunnah,* however, is not translated into English in its entirety, and many find it dissatisfying due to lack of detail. Besides this point, some question the qualifications of the author, and this is a point of contention.

As mentioned above, the only fundamental books of any of the Madhhabs, to date, to combine fairly comprehensive information with excellence of translation are those of Nuh Ha Mim Keller (*Al-Nawawi's Manual of Islam* and *Reliance of the Traveler*). And although Nuh Keller has come under considerable criticism for his ties with Sufism and promotion of Ashari *aqeeda,* as well as for certain comments he makes in the books of his translation, his books are widely respected for accuracy of translation. Fortunate it is, then, that Keller's personal comments are denoted by a small 'n' preceding each comment, for it is important that the reader be able to differentiate the translation, which is well respected, from Keller's personal comments, which are not. His criticism of Shaykh al-Islam Ibn Taymeeyah, in particular, is to be expected given the fact that Ibn Taymeeyah was at war with the very schools of *aqeeda* and Sufism to which Keller adheres. Keller's notes regarding Sufism and *aqeeda* are equally predictable and reflect his bias on these subjects.

Argument for or against the Madhhabs, Salafi vs. Ashari or Maturidi *aqeeda*, Sayyid Saabiq, Nuh Keller, and even for or against the methodology of attempting to re-derive *fiqh* through personal analysis of Qur'an and hadith (a discipline recognized by scholars as being the territory of scholars, and scholars alone) are plentiful and readily available through Islamic bookstores and on the internet. For the benefit of the reader, however, I will just state that one of the most excellent treatises regarding the Madhhabs is the short article, *Understanding The Four Madhhabs*, by Abdal Hakim Murad (a.k.a. Abdal Hakim Winter, a.k.a. T. J. Winter), a most eloquent author, although himself a controversial figure in his own right. This article also is readily available through Islamic bookstores and on the internet.

3) The Practice

Once converts embrace Islam through proclaiming the *shahada*, the pillars of Islam become incumbent upon them, as discussed above. Learning and implementing these pillars becomes the keystone upon which a person's religion depends, and is facilitated by selecting and following one of the respected *fiqh* schools of Sunni Islam.[24] Should a person incline towards the Madhhabs, the general teaching is not to consider any one Madhhab better than the others, but rather to consider all four of the Madhhabs to be of equivalent excellence, and to devote oneself to the teachings of whichever Madhhab is most readily available. For most Muslims in America and England the Shafi Madhhab proves the most easily learned, simply because the books of the other Madhhabs have not been translated into the English language with the same degree of excellence.[25]

Books promoted through 'Salafi,' or 'Qur'an and Sunnah' societies are also generally of significant value, for they are frequently of useful content, convenient size, and competent scholarship. Many others, however, embody substandard scholarship and reflect the opinions of the author more than the understanding of the *ulema*. So a person has to trust to the guidance of Allah and to the recommendations of respected brothers and sisters in faith, while at the same time remaining both selective and critical.

On the other hand, many new converts elect to follow the teachings of whatever *imam* or scholar is closest at hand, usually meaning the *imam* of the local mosque. Depending on the individuals involved, this may or may not be a successful formula, for most *imams* in the West lack the qualifications of scholarship, more than a few are corrupt, and many are misleading, whether intentionally or out of ignorance. The new convert would do well to keep this in mind, and hold fast to the teachings of traditional and respected scholars whose record of excellence precedes them.

One painfully common error is to trust the opinion of any and all 'ethnic' Muslims, meaning those born into Islam. This may come as a shock to new converts, but 'ethnic' Muslims in the West are frequently the *worst* representatives of Islam. In fact, these Muslims frequently give Islam a bad name, and rather than helping the new Muslim converts, make life in their new religion confusing or difficult. This, of course, is not true in all cases, but it is encountered frequently enough to warrant mention.

There may be many reasons why 'ethnic' Muslims fall short of being the best examples, but not the least is the fact that many of these Muslims come to the West for a purpose, and that purpose is frequently anything but religion. To put it bluntly, many 'ethnic' Muslims make *hijra* from the land of the Muslims to the land of the disbelievers in search of *dunia* (the material things of this world). These are Muslims who have set priority on the *dunia* over the religion, compromising the one for the other, and so they cannot be expected to be among the best representatives of Islam. In fact, many left the religion of Islam when they left the shores of their countries if, that is, they ever were practicing Muslims to begin with. And many weren't. To be

---

[24] Without following blindly, and without going to extremes.
[25] See the aforementioned books of Shafi *fiqh*, as translated by Nuh Ha Mim Keller.

fair, however, some individuals encounter such difficulties as to motivate a return to the religion, and a certain percentage of these actually become better Muslims than those they left behind in their native lands. And then again, many good Muslims have emigrated to America, England or Europe in order to escape persecution in their home lands, simply because they were the best and most practicing of Muslims in a country that persecuted practicing Muslims. So the mixture of 'ethnic' Muslims is really a colorful collage of religious profiles, ranging from some of the worst to some of the best.

The new convert just shouldn't expect them all to be saints or angels. Only a fractionally small minority come anywhere close.

Likewise, the new convert must expect a certain degree of hardship upon entering Islam. Converts frequently observe that they seemed to suffer tests of faith upon converting to Islam, and frequently these tests seem to involve whatever it was that a convert gave priority to in life before Islam. Whether a matter of health, wealth, spouses, children, or whatever, the new convert can expect to be tested, for hardship is the test of sincerity. Some pass, some fail, and in the end these tests tend to weed out the insincere from the healthy crop of true and sincere believers.

The good news is that the believer suffers nothing in the path of Allah but that Allah will compensate for it, either in this world or in the next, and manifold times the value of whatever was forsaken for His pleasure. So, as Muhammad ﷺ counseled those who converted in his day, the convert in the present day should also be counseled to expect and prepare for hardship for, as Muhammad ﷺ related, "Whoever Allah wants good for, he tests them."[26] Following such tests and trials the Muslim can be assured of receiving recompense for remaining patient and steadfast upon the truth, for Muhammad ﷺ also taught,

> "There is not a thing which afflicts the believer, even the thorn which pricks him, except that Allah writes for him, because of that, a good deed and removes from him a bad deed."[27]

and

> "There is nothing which afflicts the believer from grief or sorrow or fatigue, even from a worry which he worries about except that Allah expiates, because of that, some of his sins."[28]

And as if that were not enough, the religion teaches that good deeds are compensated on the scale of ten to seven hundred times the value of the good deed, at the discretion of Allah Most High, as per the hadith,

> "...he who has intended a good deed and has not done it, Allah writes it down with Himself as a full good deed, but if he has intended it and

---

[26] Bukhari (5321), Malik (1684), Ahmad (7234)
[27] Bukhari (5317), Muslim (2572)
[28] Tirmidhi (966)

has done it, Allah writes it down with Himself as from ten good deeds to seven hundred times, or many times over.*"[29]

This does not mean, however, that the Muslim should seek trials and tribulations, or make life difficult for oneself. There is no monasticism in Islam, and Muslims are encouraged to make their lives easy for themselves. Fortunately, the minimal religious obligations are easily satisfied. Should Muslims perceive themselves unable to fulfill one or more of the pillars of Islam, this usually reflects failure to recognize a dispensation which could be applied, rather than an inflexibility in the religion. Islam is simply not that rigid and uncompromising. For example, when required a person can pray sitting, or even lying down if need be. The person who is unable to fast Ramadan can make up the lost days later, or can compensate by feeding the poor. The man or woman physically unable to make *haj* can hire someone to go in their place. So Muslims who consider themselves unable to satisfy one or more of the pillars of Islam typically fail to understand the flexibilities of Islamic practice which can accommodate all circumstances of the human condition.

This is an important point, for many new Muslims attempt to implement Islam in their lives too rigidly, at times with such zeal and rigidity as to bring the predictable result of overwhelming themselves and alienating others. Three words – don't do that. The Messenger of Allah, Muhammad☆, taught, "Verily this religion is one of ease, and no one is harsh on themselves with the *deen* except that it overcomes him. So take the proper steps, approach, and have glad tidings, and seek help through prayer in the morning and the evening, as well as a bit of prayer at night."[30] Furthermore, Muhammad☆ conveyed (repeating the teaching three times for emphasis), "Verily, extremists are destroyed."[31]

The new Muslim, then, needs to implement Islam fully but gently, and ease into the subsidiary practices of Islam. If I could recommend some practical do's and don't's, they would be these:

1) Do avoid extremes. Concentrate on learning the fundamentals of the religion, and focus on learning the acceptable, alternative ways of doing things when need be. Learn about dispensations and the conditions for taking them[32] for, as stated above, the flexibility of Islam is a blessing. And don't be rigid and inflexible, either with yourself or with others, for if you are, sooner or later something will break. With regard to ourselves, Muhammad☆ cautioned Muslims to, "Take a moderate path, for whoever tries to overburden himself in the religion will be defeated."[33] Another narration relates, "This religion is easy, and whoever tries to overburden himself in the religion will be

---

* For the sake of completeness, as well as to illustrate the Mercy and Fairness of Allah Most High, the hadith continues, "But if he has intended a bad deed and has not done it, Allah writes it down with Himself as a full good deed, but if he has intended it and has done it, Allah writes it down as one bad deed."

[29] Bukhari (6126), Muslim (206)
[30] Bukhari (31)
[31] Muslim (2670)
[32] See *Reliance of the Traveler*, by Nuh Ha Mim Keller, Amana Publications, sections c6.2-6.5 and w.14.
[33] Ahmad (4/422)

defeated. Be moderate and try to perfect your action as much as you are able ...."[34] Regarding our treatment of others, even Muhammadﷺ was counseled by Allah to the effect, "It is part of the Mercy of Allah that you deal gently with them. If you were severe or harsh-hearted, they would have broken away from about you: so pass over (their faults), and ask for (Allah's) forgiveness for them; and consult them in affairs (of moment)." (TMQ – Abdullah Yusuf Ali – 3:159)

2) Do look for the middle path in all things. Islam is the religion of the middle path. If searched for, even harsh, seemingly uncompromising mandates can be understood to be the middle path between even worse extremes.

3) Do adopt modesty and humility, and learn the *adab* (manners) of Islam as early as possible -- not only for your own sake, but also for the sake of family, friends and coworkers. Brothers and sisters in Islam may excuse initial errors in religion and manners, but friends and family likely won't. They will probably be watching you from day one, and the best impression will be conveyed by presenting the best of manners. Stressing the importance of this point, Muhammadﷺ conveyed, "I have only been sent to perfect manners."[35]

4) At least to begin with, don't argue. New converts usually do not have the intellectual tools for religious debate, and would best serve the cause of Islamic *dawa* not by talking about it, but by passing on some of the same books, literature or tapes which first swayed their own hearts and minds. Beyond that, be patient, set a good example, and present Islam in the best of ways.

5) Do stay close to the mosque and the Islamic community. The strength and insights from the brothers and sisters of faith can prove invaluable and supportive. On the other hand, nonbelievers among friends and family frequently attempt to return a person from Islam, and may weaken a person's resolve. Don't compromise your religion for anyone, for to do so would constitute *kufr* (disbelief).

6) If weakened in *emaan* (faith), as many converts are at times, always return to the *shahada* and ask yourself if you believe that there is none to be worshipped but Allah, and that Muhammadﷺ was His final messenger. If so, rely upon your faith, for Allah is sufficient for the believers, and upon Him do all believers place their trust.

7) Gently ease yourself into the subsidiary practices of Islam, such as the *sunna* prayers and fasting. These extra acts of worship shelter a believer from disbelief, for everyone experiences fluctuations in *emaan*, and when a downswing occurs, those who have been practicing the subsidiary prayers and fasting may find themselves losing one or more of their voluntary prayers or fasts, but *inshallah* they won't lose the required acts of worship. On the other hand, those performing only the bare minimum have nothing to give up but the required, and should they do so in a moment of weakness, compromise the obligatory acts of worship. As one teacher put it, "If you give up the *sunna*

---

[34] Bukhari (39), An-Nisa'ee (8/121)
[35] Ahmad (8939), Bukhari in *Al-Adab Al-Mufrad* (273), Malik (1609).

(subsidiary acts of worship), eventually you will give up the *fard* (obligatory acts)."

8) Do stick with the mainstream Sunni Muslims, also known as the *Ahlus-Sunnah wal Jamah* (i.e., the group of people upon the Sunnah). As quoted above, Muhammad☗ conveyed the teaching that, "There will always be a group of my *ummah* (i.e., nation) openly on the truth until the Day of Judgment."[36] And who are the *ummah* on the truth? When asked this question a long list of some of the greatest scholars of Islam (to include Imam Ahmad, Imam Bukhari, Ali Ibn Al-Madeeni [the greatest scholar in the defects of hadith], Yahya Ibn Ma'een [the greatest scholar concerning the ranking of hadith narrators], Ibn Al-Mubarak, Sufyan At-Thauri, and many others) answered that the *ummah* upon the truth referred to the followers of hadith. In other words, those of the *Ahlus-Sunnah wal Jamah*. A supportive hadith is the one in which Muhammad☗was recorded as having taught, "Verily he among you who lives [long] will see great controversy, so you must keep to my *sunna** and to the *sunna* of the rightly-guided [Rashidite**] Caliphs – cling to them stubbornly. Beware of newly invented matters, for every invented matter is an innovation and every innovation is a going astray."[37]

9) Learn to read the Qur'an in Arabic. Even lacking understanding of the Arabic, simply reciting Qur'an can be a source of comfort, peace, and satisfaction.

10) Learn Arabic. As the Qur'an and Hadith are the doorway to Islam, Arabic is the doorway to appreciation and understanding of the Qur'an and Hadith.

11) Explore the Muslim world, when possible. Should the opportunity become available, seriously explore the possibility of making *hijra* (emigration) to one of the lands of the Muslims. However, such an emigration should not be taken lightly, for many Western converts have been severely disappointed by the shortcomings of life and religion in Muslim countries. Consider this step carefully, and begin with on-site visits, if possible. And remember that just as most ethnic Muslims are far from being saints, Muslim lands are likewise frequently far from being Islamic. However, these are the lands of our brothers and sisters in faith, and the compensation of living amongst them and contributing to their society usually offsets any difficulties. And in any case, life as a Muslim, *hijra* included, was never meant to be without trial.

12) Seek to find a way in which you can best serve Allah. Living life as a Muslim without a goal or purpose beyond making the five prayers and fasting Ramadan can be a shallow and disappointing plane of existence. Many Muslims aspire to greater achievement, and when they find their niche within the religion begin to experience the real richness of faith. One person might study, another might call to Islam,

---

[36] Bukhari (3441), Muslim (156), Abu Dawud (4252), Tirmidhi (2229)
* Meaning the words, deeds, implied consents, and appearance of the Prophet as conveyed through hadith.
** This is the title of the first four Islamic Caliphs (i.e., Abu Bakr, Umar, Uthman and Ali).
[37] Tirmidhi (2676)

another might join social outreach programs or give time to the community. Whatever a person chooses to do, know that a gift to Allah brings both immediate and future rewards, and that can be the true cement that completes and seals a person's faith.

4) Ihsaan (God-consciousness)

From the Gabriel hadith, as quoted in Chapter 2 above, we come to learn the meanings of *Islam, Emaan*, and *Ihsaan*. Those who have read *The First and Final Commandment* may have noticed that the skeletal structure of the book was based on the six integrals of Islamic faith, as defined by this hadith (i.e., belief in Allah, the angels, the books of revelation, His messengers, the Day of Judgment, and Divine Decree). This structure was intentional, for the conclusion of the Gabriel hadith was that the angel of revelation, Gabriel, had been sent to teach the critical elements of the Islamic religion. What better template, then, to follow in the teaching of religion?

Islam was discussed in *The First and Final Commandment*, and the elements of *Emaan*, being the pillars of faith, were briefly commented upon in chapter 2 of this present book. That leaves discussion of *Ihsaan* to complete the teachings of the Gabriel hadith.

Ihsaan, as per the hadith, is, "...that you worship Allah as if you see Him, and even though you do not see Him, [you know] He sees you." *Ihsaan* is God-consciousness, in all things and at all times. Perfection of *Ihsaan* leads to perfection of religion and worship, for the person of *Ihsaan* is acutely aware that his or her every thought, word and action is known to Allah, and recorded. Hence, the person of *Ihsaan* will never compromise the duties of the religion, for even when alone as regards other humans, the person of *Ihsaan* is aware of both the recording angels and the omniscience of Allah.

So how do people develop and perfect their *Ihsaan*? God-consciousness grows with certainty of faith, which itself follows from religious education in combination with temporal and spiritual experience. And this is where things get tricky.

The value of religious education is obvious; the worldly experience from living the religion expected. But spiritual experience? This is where many Muslims go around the bend. Which leads us to a discussion of Sufism.

5) Sufism

Sufism can be a confusing issue for a new convert. Initiates to Islam commonly investigate a wide variety of groups, with Sufis being one of the more immediately likeable and attractive, partially due to their high hospitality, warm and welcoming personalities, but primarily due to the accommodating flexibility with which they implement (and some groups have gone so far as to have actually modified) their religion. Furthermore, many individuals seem to have virtually an innate predilection for paths that focus their teachings and aspirations upon spiritualism.

The fact of the matter is that anyone who follows the truth of Allah is bound to experience spiritualism on some level, for those who incur the pleasure of Allah rightfully expect Allah to provide understanding and insight to His sincere servants. Two hadiths teach,

> Allah, the Exalted has said, "Whoever shows enmity to a friend of Mine, I shall be at war with him. My slave (i.e., the believing Muslim) does not draw near to Me with anything more loved by Me than the religious duties I have imposed upon him, and My slave continues to draw near to Me with supererogatory works so that I shall love him. Then when I love him I am his hearing with which he hears, his seeing with which he sees, his hand with which he holds, and his foot with which he walks. Were he to ask [something] of Me, I would surely give it to him, and were he to ask Me for refuge, I would surely grant him it."[38]

And,

> Allah the Mighty and Exalted has said "I am with my servant when he remembers me. If he remembers me to himself, then I remember him to myself. And if he mentions me in a gathering, then I mention him in a gathering of those better than them. And if he were to approach me by a hand-span then I would approach him by a cubit. And if he were to approach me by a cubit, then I would approach him by an arm's length. And if he were to come to me walking, then I would come to him running."[39]

From these teachings, Muslims understand that the more they exert themselves for the pleasure of Allah, the greater the reward and closeness to Allah. So, once a person commits to the teachings of Allah, a person's actions may be rewarded in more spheres than one.[40] Periods of both ease and tribulation are to be encountered in this worldly life, but both conditions seem to be accompanied by heightened spiritual consciousness in those Muslims confirmed in certainty and commitment to their faith.

---

[38] Bukhari (6137)

[39] Bukhari (6970), Muslim (2675), Ahmad (7416), Ibn Majah (3792, 3822)

[40] This is not to say, as many Jews and Christians do, that a pious person's reward will necessarily be found in this present life. Allah may choose to test the pious with hardship in this temporal life, reserving reward until the afterlife. Hence, the prophets and many of Allah's favorites lived difficult lives in this temporal existence, but received the greater rewards of Paradise in the life to follow.

The difference between non-Sufi Muslims and Sufis, in this regard, seems to be one of orientation. Non-Sufis tend to focus their efforts on learning the creed (aqeeda), laws (fiqh), manners (adab), and practical limits of the Islamic religion, so as to ensure correctness of belief and practice. These Muslims live their religion to the fullest, seeking the pleasure and reward of Allah Most High, fearing His punishment, and simply out of love of Him. Heightened spiritual awareness may follow in consequence, but is not an objective per se. Rather, focus is squarely centered upon correctness of aqeeda (creed), ibada (worship), and practice, for these stand to incur the pleasure of Allah and bring salvation. Lacking correctness of aqeeda, ibada, and practice, no depth of mysticism will bring salvation. So non-Sufi Muslims simply commit to the religion, study, and practice in accordance with the most respected of sources (which is to say the Qur'an, Sunnah, and interpretation thereof by respected scholars). By this pathway the soul is purified, with heightened spirituality being a predictable consequence, although not the primary objective.

Sufis, on the other hand, frequently seem diverted from the study and practice of the tenets of Islam by efforts to achieve greater mystical experiences and spiritual highs. Those who focus primarily upon mysticism are prone to sacrifice the critical correctness of aqeeda and the correct practice of the pillars of Islam, commonly resulting in the compromise, and frequently even the invalidation, of their claim to Islam. At the mildest infraction many (if not most or even all) Sufis tend towards innovation in the religion. Remembering the general principle that every act of worship is forbidden except that which has been prescribed, a person can come to understand why Ibn Masood (one of the greatest of the sahabi) cautioned:

> "Follow, do not innovate, for verily you have been given something [i.e., the religion of Islam] that is sufficient."[41]

and

> "Moderation in following the Sunna is better than exerting yourself in the bida (i.e., innovation)."[42]

Ibn Umar (another of the famous sahabi) is recorded as having reinforced this teaching with, "Every innovation is a misguidance, even if the people see it as something good."[43]

A longer, but very illustrative, story may help to summarize the above. In this tradition, Abu Musa Al-Ashari is recorded as having said to Ibn Masood,

> "Verily, I saw in the mosque a group of people sitting in circles waiting for prayer. In every circle there is a leader and with every group there are pebbles and this leader says to them, "Say 'Allahu Akbar' (i.e., Allah is the Most Great) 100 times," so they say "Allahu Akbar" 100 times (using the pebbles to count); and he says to them, "Say 'La ilaha il Allah' (i.e., there is no god worthy of worship but Allah) 100 times," and so they say "La ilaha il Allah" 100 times (using

---

[41] Darami (205)
[42] Bayhaqi (4522), Darami (223)
[43] Allalaka'i, I'tiqad Ahlus-Sunnah Wal Jamah (126)

the pebbles to count); and he says to them "Say *'Subhanallah'* (i.e., Glory be to Allah) 100 times," and so they say *"Subhanallah"* 100 times (using the pebbles to count). So Ibn Masood replied to Abu Musa, "Didn't you order them to count their sins and guarantee that none of their good deeds will be lost?" Then he (Ibn Masood) came and stood beside one of these circles and said, "What is this that I see you doing? They replied, "Oh, father of Abdur-Rahman, pebbles -- we count with them our *takbir* (*Allahu Akbar*), our *tahlil* (*La ilaha il Allah*), our *tasbih* (*Subhanallah*) and our *tahmid* (*Al humdulillah* [i.e., all praise be to Allah])."

He replied, "Count your sins. I guarantee you that none of your good actions will be lost. Woe to you, O nation of Muhammad ﷺ, how fast your destruction is! The prophet's companions are in abundance, and his clothes have not yet dried and his utensils have not been broken.* By He in Whose hands my soul is (i.e., Allah), verily you are on a guidance better than the guidance of Muhammad ﷺ** or you are opening the door to misguidance (i.e., *bida*—innovation in religion).

They replied, "By Allah, O the father of Abdur-Rahman, we only intended that which is good."

Ibn Masood replied, "And how many do intend good but do not hit the target (i.e., do not achieve it)."

Then he said that, "The prophet ﷺ said to us that, 'A group (of my *ummah*) will read the Qur'an and it will not go past their throats (meaning it will not enter their hearts).' And by Allah, I do not know, but it may be that a lot of you are from that group."

And then he left them.

One of the reporters of this hadith said, "We found a lot of those people who were in these circles fighting us on the day of *An-Nahrawan* with the Khawaraj (a battle in which Ali ibn Talib, the fourth caliph, led the Muslims against the Khawaraj, the first group of deviant Muslims, of whose ranks some of those described above had joined). [44]

From this narration, we learn that the symptoms of deviancy can sometimes be very small, but the consequences tragic. And for what? To attempt something perceived to be good which, nonetheless, 'misses the target?' The importance of adhering to the Sunnah is stressed, for as Muhammad ﷺ is recorded as having taught, "There has been nothing left which brings you closer to paradise and takes you further from the hellfire except that it has been shown to you."[45] And yet, Sufis tend to seek after ways and means by which to enhance their worship, risking trespass against the limits set by Allah Most High, and more often than not slipping into innovation.

Perhaps a historical footnote should be reviewed at this point. The origin of this term 'Sufi' is not terribly important, for the word 'Sufi' is devoid of mention either in Qur'an or Sunnah, and as such the label opens the door to sectarianism, which Allah

---

* Meaning that Muhammad ﷺ just recently died.
** In this way he mocks them with sarcasm.
[44] Darami (204)
[45] Tabarani, *Al-Kabir* (1647)

condemns (see TMQ 6:159 and 42:13). All the same, the term 'Sufi' seems to have taken root in the practice of early ascetics of wearing wool, which is known as '*Suf*' in Arabic. These early ascetics had renounced the pleasures of this world, to the degree where they were forced by poverty to wear wool -- an unpopular, irritating and swelteringly hot material in the harsh heat of the Middle East (unlike their Christian counterpart, who wore horsehair shirts out of conviction that worldly suffering equated to penance, the Sufis of Islam were simply too poor to be able to afford anything better suited to the environment than wool). Some may be impressed by such indicators of rigor and devotion, but others note that Islam is not a religion of asceticism, for self-inflicted poverty and suffering are neither prescribed nor condoned, if avoidable. As a matter of fact, Muslims are encouraged to be productive and to earn a livelihood. Muhammad taught, "Verily, the best of what you have eaten from are your earnings."[46] When asked which type of earnings are the most virtuous, the messenger of Allah replied, "The work of a man with his own hands, and every honest sale."[47] Furthermore, Abu ad-Dardaa is recorded as having commented, "Improvement of one's livelihood is from the improvement of one's *deen*, and the improvement of one's *deen* is from the improvement of one's intellect."[48]

Be that as it may, Sufis came to be associated with asceticism and spiritualism, and with time prominent Sufis came to be considered as saints by the laity who formed their following. Each such group eventually became known as a Sufi *tariqa*, or path, in which specific spiritual teachings were formalized. *Tariqas* vary greatly, and it is not possible to paint all *tariqas* with the same brush – Sufi *aqeeda*, *ibada*, and practices vary greatly from one group to another, covering the range from correctness, to *bida* (innovation), and all the way on to *kufr* (disbelief). On one hand, a small minority of Sufis are entirely mainstream. However, the more common situation is one in which Sufis compromise the laws of Islam for aberrant beliefs and practices.

The failing of Sufism lies in the transition from the Sufism of old to the Sufism of present. The original Sufis may have been pious Muslims who were subjects of poverty and deprivation due to having focused their efforts on worship, forsaking all other pursuits, including that of improving worldly position or, for that matter, even earning a living. Over a very brief period of time, however, deviant *tariqas* formed, either disoriented around the peculiar teachings of an equally peculiar, though charismatic, leader, or subsequently diverging from mainstream teachings under the pressures of misguidance.

Hence, those who subscribe to *tariqas* commit to a dangerous path in which few *tariqas* are Islamically safe in the present age, and from which few adherents ever return to correctness. Nonetheless, the siren song of mysticism and spirituality proves irresistible to many who, ungrounded in the protective *fiqh* of Islam, may be easily deceived and misled -- a phenomenon which is yet one more trend common to the three religions of Judaism, Christianity and Islam.

In all three religions, those who seek spiritual paths in primacy over adherence to the strictness of the law tend to stray, for they are more drawn to the spiritual teachings of

---

[46] Tirmidhi (1358), Ibn Majah (2290)

[47] Bayhaqi (10177)

[48] Jami' Bayan al Ilm

'saints' and charismatic leaders than to the straight path of Allah's design, as conveyed through His revelation and through the example of the prophets. Within the Islamic religion, such adherents typically fall into one of two camps, the first being the misguided followers whose ignorance is betrayed by lack of knowledge of basic (and protective) Islamic teachings. The second camp of adherents, paradoxically, are surprisingly well educated on Islamic principles and sciences, and may even be considered scholars in certain fields of study. Frequently these individuals practice Islam with an impressive rigor, taking the most difficult and cautious path in all things religious, excepting Sufism, that is. Peculiarly enough, aside from the mysticisms of Sufism, the discipline in which these scholarly Sufis tend to relax their exacting standards most is typically in the most critical field of *aqeeda*. They may be scholars in *fiqh*, and yet adhere to salvation-threatening deviancies of creed.

A whole slew of deviancies has resulted, the most dangerous of which involve *shirk* or *kufr*. Some *tariqas* have elevated the status of Muhammadﷺ beyond his earthly humanity, others have deified their sheiks. Of lesser, but still serious concern is the relaxing of Islamic standards in the interest of greater permissibility, often under the guise of modernization.

And none of this should come as a surprise. The history of religion exposes the tendency of man to drift from the laws of Allah to paths of greater permissiveness, especially when such paths are beautified by claims of spiritual exclusivity. Just as the strict and demanding laws of Orthodox Judaism gave way to the lenient mysticism of Reform Judaism, Christianity suffered a transformation from the Old Testament laws of Unitarian origins to the indulgent mysticisms of the Gnostics, of whom Trinitarian Christians form a subset (as discussed in *The First and Final Commandment*). Deviant sects (most of them Sufi) claiming the banner of Islam have continued this disturbing tradition of increasing permissiveness, in conflict with the clear and present laws of Islam.

I would close this section with the following observations:
1) Most who seek a spiritual path do so aspiring to be a *wali*, or 'friend of Allah,' which Sufis conceive to imply the status of sainthood, complete with mystical abilities. Such Sufis are preoccupied by the desire to achieve heightened spiritual status, and conceive that the correct manner by which to attain such status is through the Sufi path. Not true. The way to become a *wali*, which as defined by Allah Most High means nothing more than a believer and one who fears Allah (TMQ 10:62-63), is simply to practice the religion of Islam as it was revealed, no more and no less.
2) Most Sufis, in my experience, exhibit bizarre personalities. Typically, it does not take long for new Muslims to recognize that something about the Sufis they meet is uncomfortably strange. Usually this relates to peculiarities in how they think, though often the matter relates more to aberrant social skills. In any case, weirdness, abnormal interactions and peculiar personal affect all seem to be common companions to Sufism, and should be taken as a warning sign.
3) Another prominent trademark of Sufis is that somewhere, somehow, they tend to compromise the faith or practice of Islam in the process of fulfilling practices of their chosen *tariqa*. For example, a person might

4) Just as some Sufis demote the importance of certain elements of the Islamic religion, others (i.e., extreme Sufis -- fortunately an underwhelming minority) go so far as to make mockery of the religion. For example, some Sufis stop praying based on a misinterpretation of the Qur'anic ayah "And worship your Lord until there comes to you the certainty" (TMQ 15:99). These Sufis claim 'the certainty' refers to certainty of faith, which they have achieved, and so they no longer need to pray. Not true. Muhammad and all previous prophets of Allah prayed until they died. Are these Sufis saying they have greater certainty of faith than the prophets of Allah? The correct interpretation of the above *ayat* is the command to pray the five daily prayers until death. The certainty of life referred to in this Qur'anic *ayat* is not certainty of faith, which some achieve and others don't, but death, which is the one certainty of all lives, and the evidence for this understanding is to be found in the *tafseers* (interpretation of the Qur'an) of Ibn Jarir at-Tabari and Ibn Kathir (the two most famous of all *tafseers*), which base this conclusion on the interpretation of the Qur'an by some of the most famous students of the *sahabi* (i.e., Salim ibn Abdullah, Mujahid, Qatada, Al Hassan al Basri, and Ibn Zayd). And none of the famous interpreters of *tafseer* from amongst the pious predecessors interpreted this verse as the extreme Sufis do.

5) As in the above example, many Sufis go astray in the same way as the Jews and Christians, for Muhammad conveyed Allah's revelation that the Jews and Christians take their rabbis and priests "as lords besides Allah." (TMQ 9:31) Furthermore, a hadith relates that Adi ibn Hatim entered upon the prophet with a silver cross on his neck. The prophet read the following verse: "They worshipped their rabbis and priests besides Allah." So Uday replied, "They do not worship them." And the prophet replied, "Yes they do. They made that which was unlawful upon them lawful, and that which was lawful upon them unlawful. So they followed them in this. And that is how they worshipped them."[49] In similar fashion, many Sufis adopt the liberal and incorrect teachings of their Sufi sheiks in preference to the clear teachings of the prophet of Allah, Muhammad, following their Sufi sheiks in unlawful matters which the Sufi sheiks have declared lawful, such as abandoning prayer. And this subject directly leads into the next, which is that:

6) Most Sufis justify their actions and beliefs with fabricated or weak hadith, or by unauthentic interpretations of Qur'an – a matter anticipated given the teaching, "It is He who has sent down to you [O Muhammad] the book; in it are verses [that are] precise – they are

---

[49] Tirmidhi (3095), Bayhaqi (20137)

the foundation of the Book – and others unspecific. As for those in whose hearts is deviation [from truth], they will follow that of it which is unspecific, seeking discord and seeking an interpretation [suitable to them]...' (TMQ 3:7).

7) And speaking of seeking interpretations 'suitable to them,' Sufis tend to be prone to exaggeration, frequently magnifying the significance of events or persons. Through this disturbing tendency, Sufis have gone so far as to have elevated the status of Muhammadﷺ, members of his family, or even 'sheiks' who claimed to have followed in his wake (within their particular *tariqa*, of course). Sometimes this leads to *shirk*, sometimes to *kufr*, and not uncommonly to both. For example, a Sufi once tried to convince me that adherents of his *tariqa* make *ibada* until they become, as he put it, "one with Allah" – a clear statement of both *shirk* and *kufr*, even if intended as a metaphor. In the Islamic religion, if a man pronounces divorce upon his wife, *even if joking*, they are divorced! In Islamic law divorce is such a serious matter that it cannot be stated even in jest except that it becomes binding! How much more serious if a person makes such statements as that above, negating the oneness of Allah, which is the most sacred of *all* truths – so sacred that salvation hangs in the balance of this one core tenet of faith?

8) Many Sufis claim a mystical chain of teaching going back to one of the *sahabi*, upon which the teachings of their *tariqa* are founded. For example, one of the Sufi 'sheikhs' in England is known by his followers as the 'fortieth link in the golden chain,' by which they imply that he is the fortieth Sufi sheikh in a chain going back to the prophet, Muhammadﷺ. Such flowery phraseology does not alter the reality, however, for these 'chains,' for the most part, cannot be traced back more than 300 years, and are filled with names of unknown and/or questionable characters with less than respectable deeds or stellar repute.

9) While there are many deviant Sufi *tariqas* in the present day, few (if any) are upon correctness. Those who embark upon this path put salvation at risk, and for what? The safest path is obvious, the Sufi path slippery and treacherous, the benefit elusive, the teachings doubtful at best and disbelief at worst. And as Muhammadﷺ counseled, "The *halal* is clear, and the *haram* is clear, but between the two are matters which are doubtful to many people. Therefore, whoever avoids these doubtful matters clears himself with regard to his religion and his honor, but he who falls into doubtful matters falls into the *haram*. [He is like] a shepherd grazing his sheep at the edge of a sanctuary, about to cross over the boundary. Truly, every king has a sanctuary, and truly Allah's sanctuary is His Prohibitions."[50] And woe to those who violate Allah's prohibitions, whether alone or on the tail of a *tariqa*.

---

[50] Bukhari (52), Muslim (1599), Abu Dawud (3329)

6) Sunnah of the *Shaitan*

The path of the pious leads a person into the contest between good and evil. Whereas the good, meaning the beliefs and practices of the religion, is taught to the new convert over and again, one of the most important subjects for the new convert is also one of the least discussed -- and that is the way of evil. And by the way of evil we mean the way (or *sunnah*) of the *Shaitan* (Satan, also known by his proper name of Iblees), whose dedicated purpose (along with his helper *shayateen* [evil jinn, or devils]) is to misguide humankind. To learn the beliefs and practices of the religion is to learn the path of piety. To learn the *sunnah*, or way, of Iblees is to 'know the enemy,' in order to protect oneself from being ambushed or led astray.

To begin with, Iblees approaches in many ways. For those already astray, he provides encouragement through making the path of impiety easy and attractive. He may choose to leave the unrighteous alone, but then again he may actually provide pleasures or even mystical experiences or apparent miracles in order to cement the misguided upon a false faith. Hence, statues may actually cry through the machinations of the *shayateen*, leading idol worshippers to greater devotion in the depths of their pagan deception. Visions of Jesus or Mary may actually be generated by Iblees or by one of his confederate *shayateen* in order to reinforce misguided faiths that recline upon articles of disbelief, such as the Trinity or the apotheosis of Jesus. Or at a lesser level, the pride of the disbeliever may be bolstered in order to reinforce confidence upon falsehood, effectively smothering the modesty required for a person to turn to the Creator with openness and sincerity.

And what is the first sin? This is a question that stumps most new converts, and many mature Muslims as well. So what is the first sin? Was it the eating of the forbidden fruit? No. No, the first sin was the sin of pride, for which Iblees was demoted from paradise. The first sin was not of Adam, but of Iblees, and the story, in brief, is this: Iblees used to be one of the pious jinn. He practiced the articles of worship with such piety as to have earned a place in the company of the angels, and in fact was assigned by Allah to oversee the lowest heaven. However, when Adam was created and the occupants of the heavens were commanded to prostrate to Adam, Iblees became prideful, conceiving himself to be better, reasoning that the jinn were made from smokeless fire, while mankind was made from clay. The Holy Qur'an relates the story as,

> And [mention] when We said to the angels, "Prostrate before Adam";
> so they prostrated, except for Iblees. He refused and was arrogant and
> became of the disbelievers. (TMQ 2:34)

In one brief line, Allah informs us that Iblees refused, the reason was pride, and the result was disbelief. How quickly a believer can fall from grace into disbelief! And for no more reason than pride, and the evil harvest it reaps. To continue the story,

> 7:12 [Allah] said, "What prevented you from prostrating when I
> commanded you?" [Satan] said, "I am better than him. You created
> me from fire and created him from clay [i.e., earth]"

7:13 [Allah] said, "Descend from it [i.e., Paradise], for it is not for you to be arrogant therein. So get out; indeed, you are of the debased."

7:14 [Satan] said, "Reprieve me until the Day they are resurrected."

7:15 [Allah] said, "Indeed, you are of those reprieved."

7:16 [Satan] said, "Because You have put me in error, I will surely sit in wait for them [i.e., mankind] on Your straight path.

7:17 Then I will come to them from before them and from behind them and on their right and on their left, and You will not find most of them grateful [to You]."

7:18 [Allah] said, "Get out of it [i.e., Paradise], reproached and expelled. Whoever follows you among them – I will surely fill Hell with you, all together."

As punishment for his pride, which obstructed obedience to Allah Most High, Iblees was cast out of Paradise. After securing Allah's reprieve until the Day of Judgment, Iblees vowed to misguide humankind from the 'straight path.' As for those who follow the misguidance of Iblees, Allah promises, "I will surely fill Hell with you, all together."

Now, fast forward to the person reading these words. What is one of the dominant characteristics of humankind, if not pride? And what barrier stands between most people and turning to God with humility in search of His truth? Answer: Pride. And how quickly can pride turn a person from belief to disbelief? From paradise to perdition? Pretty darn quick – see above.

What other weaknesses of human nature provide fault-lines through which the *Shaitan* can leverage disobedience to the Creator? Envy is one. Greed another. Desire, despair, dissatisfaction, impatience, sexual passion and anger a few more. Even contentment, if permitted to lull a person into inaction. And pride. At the beginning, at the end, and at all points between.

Let's look at how this can work. To begin with, Iblees, the *Shaitan*, has priorities. First he will try to get people to commit *kufr*, or disbelief. If he cannot get people to commit major *shirk*, he will try to get them to commit minor *shirk*. Failing that, he will try to lead people to commit innovation (*bida*). Should that fail, he will try to get people to commit major sins, and if unable, then minor sins. But what if he cannot get a person to commit even a minor sin? Then perhaps the *Shaitan* will try to invalidate a good deed, for example by injecting a sense of pride, by making a person inclined to showing off, or by motivating a person through greed to seek worldly gain rather than the pleasure of Allah. All of these motivations may lead to Allah refusing to accept a person's good deeds. To drive the point home, Muhammad ﷺ taught that the first three people to enter the Hellfire on the Day of Judgment are a scholar, a charitable man, and a martyr who dedicated their actions to other than Allah. The hadith is a follows:

Abu Hurayrah narrated that the Prophet繁 said: "Indeed, Allah the Most Exalted will descend to His slaves on the Day of Judgment, and judge between them. All the nations will humble to their knees (kneeling). The first people to be called to account on the Day of Judgment will be [a scholar] and reciter of the Qur'an, and a martyr who was slain in the cause of Allah, and a rich person (who used to constantly give his wealth). Allah will ask [the scholar] and reciter of the Qur'an: 'Have I not taught you what was revealed to my Messenger?' And he will answer, 'Yes.' So Allah will ask him, 'What did you do with that which I taught you?' He will respond, 'I used to recite it day in and day out [and I used to seek knowledge and teach it to the people].' Then Allah will answer him, 'No, you have lied!' and the angels will say, 'No, you have lied!' Allah will then say, 'You only wished for people to say about you: He is a [scholar and] reciter of the Qur'an, and so it was said!' And the person with great wealth will be brought forth, and Allah will say, 'Did I not bless you so that you did not need to depend on others?' He will respond, 'Yes!' Allah will ask, 'Then what did you do with what I had given you?' He will say, 'I fulfilled my family obligations, and spent my money in charity.' Then Allah will say, 'No, you have lied!' and the angels will say, 'No, you have lied!' Allah will then say, 'You only spent so that people would call you generous, and so it was said!' And the person who died in the way of Allah will be asked, 'How did you die?' He will answer, 'O my Lord! I was ordered to make Jihad in your way, so I fought until I was killed!' Allah will say, 'No, you have lied!' and the angels will say, 'No, you have lied!' Allah will then say, 'You only fought so that it would be said of you: He has great valor, and so it has been said!' Then, the Prophet繁 tapped my knee and said: 'O Abu Hurayrah! These are the first three people amongst the creation of Allah that the fire of Hell will consume on the Day of Judgment!'"[51]

The point is that good deeds, if dedicated to other than Allah, stand to be rejected – yet another example of actions judged by intentions. And if the scholars, the charitable, and the martyrs are not safe from misdirected intentions, then who is?

If all else fails, Iblees may try to soothe a person to complacence, for a feeling of well being (the overconfident belief of having done enough of good deeds) can be the first step to turning a person away from the height of piety. Those who cannot be brought to ruin completely, Iblees may try to bring down notch by notch.

But if a person persists on the path of righteousness, even then the *Shaitan* does not give up, for he can still have an impact by distracting a person from good deeds of greater worth to performing good deeds of lesser worth. After all, there are only so many hours in the day.

So a person must be vigilant, and not despair. Knowing that a life of piety equates to a life of struggle against the forces of evil, in which Iblees plays a person off the combination of external temptations and internal desires, helps a person to prepare for

---

[51] Muslim (1905), Tirmidhi (2382), Nasaa'i (3137)

the struggle. Knowing that Iblees never quits until the soul leaves the body helps a person commit to patience and steadfastness. And knowing that Allah created humankind imperfect helps a person to avoid despair, for the test of a person's faith in the beneficence of Allah lies not in attaining the unobtainable (i.e., perfection), but rather in relying upon Allah to accept *tawbah* (repentance) when error *is* made. The problem with failing to recognize the human tendency to err is that such people see religion like dieting. Once they violate a diet by so much as an extra leaf of lettuce, they figure they've ruined it, it's all over, might as well finish off the box of cookies and pint of Fudge Royale as well. This may be the way of diets, but it is not the way of religion, for in the words of Yaqoob (Jacob), "Indeed, no one despairs of relief from Allah except the disbelieving people." (TMQ 12:87)

The fact of the matter is that Allah could have created humankind free of error, like the angels. However, unlike the angels humans were given free will, with the point of our existence being to serve and worship Allah *voluntarily*, and to return to Allah in repentance when in error.

For some, however, this is not enough. For some, life is governed by a constant search for greater significance in existence. These individuals are frequently drawn to mysticism, because through mysticism they feel they achieve heightened spiritual awareness and closer proximity to Allah. Enter the *Shaitan* once again. Having already discussed the first sin of Iblees, what was the first sin of Adam? Everybody knows the story of eating from the tree of forbidden fruit, but why, exactly, did Adam do it? What was his motivation? We find the answer in the Qur'an, Surah 7, Ayah 20-21, where Iblees was recorded as having advised Adam,

> "Your Lord did not forbid you this tree except that you become angels or become of the immortal." And he swore [by Allah] to them, "Indeed, I am to you from among the sincere advisors."

And Adam believed him. Despite the fact that Allah had previously warned Adam against Iblees (When Allah called to Adam, he posed the rhetorical question, "Did I not forbid you from that tree and tell you that Satan is to you a clear enemy?" TMQ 7:22). All of which can reasonably lead a person to suggest that the nature of man, from the very beginning, is such that his sense of reason can be overpowered by his lust for higher spiritual states (i.e., that of the angels or 'of the immortal'). And the *Shaitan* continues to play off this weakness in many Muslims, as he did with Adam.

And like Adam, the Muslims have been warned.

Nonetheless, throughout time there have always been those eager to bite the apple of mysticism and apotheosis. Some were so enthusiastic as to go overboard in religion, ascribing divinity to elements of Allah's creation. One sect of Jews used to consider Uzair (Ezra) the Son of God, many Christians revere Christ Jesus as either the Son of God or as partner in divinity, and some members of extreme Shi'ites have gone so far as to have deified Ali. Larger groups, however, achieved misdirection from the laws of Judaism, Christianity, and Islam through the Reform, Gnostic, and Sufi movements, respectively, as previously discussed. The fact that these trends are shared between all three of these Abrahamic faiths suggests that Iblees has found an approach to misguidance that works, and has kept repeating it throughout the religions, and throughout the ages -- "Embrace mysticism, leave the law; embrace mysticism, leave the law; I'm your sincere advisor."

7) Sincere Advisors

Callers to misguidance have many faces and enter through many doors, but almost always present themselves as sincere advisors. The challenge for all Muslims is to learn correctness of Islamic belief and practices, for this establishes the rule by which deviant individuals and groups may be known and measured. Conversely, hints can be gained from those who oppose the Islamic religion, for a person can fairly assume that antagonists of the religion will not support individuals or groups that represent true Islam. So when anti-Islamic interest groups endorse a particular sect or ideology under the guise of "Islam," Muslims should regard such an endorsement more with condemnation than approval.

Any of the publications of the Western military establishment or governmental think-tanks expose the relevant prejudices, as does the Western media, which is recognizably slanted toward non-Islamic party concerns. Cheryl Benard's *Civil Democratic Islam* (available on the website, www.Rand.org), from the National Security Research Division of the Rand Corporation, one of the foremost Western policy think-tanks, can be used as an informative example.

Benard's treatise begins with the statement,

> "There is no question that contemporary Islam is in a volatile state, engaged in an internal and external struggle over its values, its identity, and its place in the world. Rival versions are contending for spiritual and political dominance. This conflict has serious costs and economic, social, political, and security implications for the rest of the world. Consequently, the West is making an increased effort to come to terms with, to understand, and to influence the outcome of this struggle."[52]

The West is "making an increased effort to...influence the outcome of this struggle"? Blunt and to the point. Obvious, as well. So, remembering that Benard's work is designed for scholars and policymakers, let's take it from there (Oh, and just to make the point that this is not some obscure treatise in policymaker circles, a search of the Rand Corporation database through their own website for the word 'Islam' produced Benard's *Civil Democratic Islam* as the first hit, sorted by relevance, as of the writing of this book).

So, to continue, Benard goes on to divide the Muslim world into four broad divisions, being fundamentalists, traditionalists, modernists, and secularists. Since the fundamentalists, by definition, are those who adhere most closely to the fundamentals of Islam, there is no surprise that they are viewed unfavorably by the author. In the words of the author, "Supporting them is not an option, except for transitory tactical considerations."[53]

Ms. Benard goes on to assert that traditionalists are not to be trusted but "The modernists and secularists are closest to the West in terms of values and policies."[54]

---

[52] Benard, Cheryl. *Civil Democratic Islam*. Rand Corporation. P. ix
[53] Benard, p. x.
[54] Benard, p. x.

The recommendation of the author, therefore, is that modernists and secularists are to be supported whereas fundamentalists are to be confronted and opposed, with traditionalists used as leverage against fundamentalists in order to wage war against the fundamentalists from two fronts – both from without and from within the religion.[55]

All of which should hint to the Muslim to have exact opposite priorities, and to follow a relatively contrary strategy.[56]

Similarly, the author recommends to "Encourage the popularity and acceptance of Sufism,"[57] which, to the Muslim, means 'don't,' as in 'Do not, do not, do not.' And for good reason. Sufis (classified in Benard's work as a subcategory of modernists[58]), modernists and secularists all take fanciful liberties in interpreting the Qur'an and Sunnah, rely upon independent and selective reasoning in vain attempts to tailor Islam closer to their hearts' desires, and steadfastly support one another while disparaging all those who advocate the methodology of the *salaf* (the pious predecessors, being the first three, and the best, generations following the revelation of the Holy Qur'an and the messengership of Muhammadﷺ).

So while the 'sincere' advisors are many, appreciation of their perspective and orientation helps to differentiate between those who should be respected, those who should be avoided, and those who should be refuted.

---

[55] The term "fundamentalist Muslims," when applied literally, refers to those who adhere to the fundamentals of Islam. However, applied colloquially, the term evokes images of militant Muslim extremists. As I understand Ms. Benard's thesis, she refers to both groups under the same title of "fundamentalism." But this is both unfair and inaccurate. In fact, true Muslim fundamentalists, meaning those Muslims who adhere to the teachings of true Islam, are quick to condemn the militant extremists and radical Muslims who have perpetuated so many crimes both against humanity and against the religion of Islam. The point is that if Ms. Benard asserts that militant Muslim extremists (fundamentalist Muslims in the colloquial sense) should be opposed, most strictly practicing Muslims (fundamentalist Muslims in the literal sense) would agree. However, if she means that strictly practicing Muslims should be opposed, then no true Muslim can agree, for dedication to Islam demands adherence to its teachings.

[56] But without falling into the error of militant extremism or, as it has come to be known, "radical Islam."

[57] Benard, p. 80.

[58] Benard, p. 62.

8) Summary

Many converts to the Islamic religion enter the faith with a profound sense of relief accompanied by the feeling of having arrived – having arrived at the truth and at the end of their religious search. To a certain extent such feelings are justified, but to a nearly equal measure a new convert's journey is just beginning. The fact of the matter is that the religion of Islam is divided into a variety of sects and paths of misguidance, the most significant of which have been touched upon in the discussion above.

In many ways I consider a good analogy to conversion to be that of arriving, after a long and difficult journey, at a major transportation hub such as Grand Central Station in New York City, Victoria Station in London, or any of the many huge train stations or international airports found scattered around the world. There is a sense of relief at having arrived – a sense of peace and satisfaction, joy even. These emotions are transient, however, for choices have to be made and the journey continued. The number of connecting paths which branch off from the central station (the station of Islam, if you will) are huge, and only one (the path of Allah's design, i.e., that which Muhammad☙ and his companions were upon) is correct. Wrong choices can usually be recovered from, but typically at a cost, and far better would it be to take the correct connection from the beginning.

Hence, the new convert must be prepared to encounter a number of choices which may at first appear confusing and controversial. Fortunately, however, the religion of Islam is easy and simple – it is not the religion that is difficult and confusing, but rather it is certain individuals who, lacking wisdom and balance, make the religion harsh and uncompromising. The result of implementing the religion in such a manner has unfortunate consequences, the least of which is confusion and discord, the greatest of which is apostasy.

Recognizing the pitfalls, believers do well to constantly turn to Allah in remembrance and trust. Whether making *tawbah* (repentance) for a transgression or seeking assistance against adversity, believers trust Allah to answer their *du'aa* (supplication) with whatever He knows to be best. As Allah Most High teaches, "I respond to the invocation of the supplicant when he calls upon Me. So let them respond to Me (by obedience) and believe in Me that they may be (rightly) guided" (TMQ 2:186). True believers never lose hope, for they have faith that as Allah has brought them this far, He will never desert them, so long as they rely upon Him, and upon Him alone. Every prayer, the Muslim renews this trust by reciting Surah *Al Fatihah* and affirming "It is You we worship and You we ask for help," following which the Muslim seeks Allah's guidance to "the straight path." *This* is the most important supplication, and the one believers trust Allah to answer.

And remember, despite the obstacles and confusion, the convert to Islam *has* arrived. The value of embracing Islam is so great that for this one leap of faith Allah has assigned His greatest reward, which is to say the reward of paradise. And for the blessings of this reward, all Muslims should strive and be grateful, appreciating the preciousness of the many blessings of Islam while purifying themselves through sincerity of intention and perfection of worship. The process of striving for correctness is what the perfection of a person's Islam is all about, and it is this effort that separates the sincere from the insincere.

And with that in mind, let us pray: May Allah guide us all, and help us to perfect and unite ourselves upon truth and righteousness, purity and piety. And may Allah grant all Muslims patience and perseverance on the correct and blessed path of His design in this life, and bless us with the peaceful bliss of paradise in the next.

Having said that, let us now do our part and *work* for it.

APPENDIX 1 – RECOMMENDED READING

Translations of the Meaning of the Holy Qur'an:

1) *The Holy Qur'an* (King Fahd Holy Qur-an Printing Complex, Al-Madinah Al-Munawarah, Saudi Arabia) and *The Qur'an* (Tahrike Tarsile Qur'an Inc., Elmhurst, New York) both present the translation of Abdullah Yusuf Ali – an excellent translation, enhanced by the beauty of more classical English than that found in more modern translations. A major shortcoming, however, is that the translator's commentary contains multiple errors, and is best avoided in favor of more classic, and respected, *tafaseer* (explanations of the meanings of the Qur'an).

2) *The Noble Qur'an* (King Fahd Holy Qur-an Printing Complex, Al-Madinah Al-Munawarah, Saudi Arabia) translated by Dr. Muhammad Al-Hilali and Dr. Muhammad Muhsin Khan. A more modern and literal translation than that of Abdullah Yusuf Ali, thoroughly researched and complemented by explanations from the tafseers of Ibn Katheer, al-Qurtubee, and at-Tabaree, as well as quotations of authentic hadith, primarily from the collection of al-Bukhari. This is without a doubt the most error-free of the English translations, yet this translation nonetheless suffers from a certain lack of fluency in the English language. Although an exceptional reference, dedicated reading can become tiresome due to the format and limitations of the language.

3) *The Qur'an* (revised and edited by Saheeh International, Abul-Qasim Publishing House, Jeddah, Saudi Arabia). An excellent, modern, easily readable and highly respected translation, thought by many to be the overall best available in the English language. Highly recommended as the first book for those seeking an easy, accurate, and pleasing translation of meaning of the Qur'an.

Sciences of the Qur'an:

1) *An Introduction to the Sciences of the Qur'aan* (Al-Hidaayah Publishing, Birmingham, England), by Abu Ammaar Yasir Qadhi.

2) *Approaching the Qur'an* (White Cloud Press), by Michael Sells

Hadith Collections:

1) *An-Nawawi's Forty Hadith*
2) *Riyadh-Us-Saliheen*
3) *Al-Lu'lu'wal-Marjan*

History (of Islam):

1) *Muhammad, His Life Based on the Earliest Sources* (The Islamic Texts Society, Cambridge, England) by Martin Lings. An excellent and comprehensive history of the life of Muhammadﷺ, only slightly marred by the few aforementioned errors (see relevant footnote, section 4.D.).

2) *When the Moon Split* (Darussalam Publishers, Riyadh, Saudi Arabia) by Safiur-Rahman Mubarakpuri. An excellent, award-winning history of the Prophetﷺ.

History (of the Arabs):

1) *A History of the Arab Peoples* (Warner Books) by Albert Hourani. Scholarly and comprehensive.

Comparative Religion (from a Muslim perspective):

1) *The First and Final Commandment* (Amana Publications), by the present author – the first book in this series. Preview through the website, www.Leveltruth.com, or purchase online through www.amana-publications.com.

2) *A Muslim Study of the Origins of the Christian Church* (Oxford University Press), by Ruqaiyyah Waris Maqsood. An extraordinary, and sadly neglected, treasure of theology written by this British scholar.

3) *The Mysteries of Jesus* (Sakina Books, Oxford), by Ruqaiyyah Waris Maqsood. Same book and author, different title.

Comparative Religion (from a non-Muslim perspective):

1) *Misquoting Jesus* (Harper San Francisco), by Bart D. Ehrman.

2) *Lost Christianities* (Oxford University Press), by Bart D. Ehrman.

3) And, for that matter, almost anything by Bart D. Ehrman. For further reading, see the footnotes to his books.

Basic Information on Islam:

1) *What Everyone Should Know About Islam and Muslims* (Kazi Publications, Chicago, IL), by Suzanne Haneef. A comprehensive, beautifully written primer.

2) *What Every Christian Should Know About Islam* (The Islamic Foundation, Markfield, England), by Ruqaiyyah Waris Maqsood. Shorter than Suzanne Haneef's book, but every bit as enjoyable and informative, with greater emphasis on theology, balanced by personal narrative.

Miscellaneous Treasures:

1) *The Road to Mecca* (Islamic Book Trust, Kuala Lumpur), by Muhammad Asad. A remarkable and heartwarming story of

one man's journey, first to Islam, and then through the world
of the Arabs.

GLOSSARY OF TERMS

Adab – Good manners

AH – After Hijra. The zero point of the Islamic calendar corresponding to the Muslim Hijra (migration) from Makkah to Medina in July of the year 622 CE (AD). Subsequent dates were calculated according to the lunar calendar, which differs from the Julian calendar by roughly 10 days each year.

Aqeeda -- Creed

Ayah – Verse of the Holy Qur'an.

Ayat – Plural of *ayah*

Bida – Innovation

BH – Before Hijra. See 'AH' for explanation.

CE – 'Common Era' or 'Christian Era,' corresponding to the same calendar and dates as 'AD.'

Dawa – Invitation

Deen – Way of life, meaning the complete code of conduct dictated by submission to the will of Allah. Frequently mistranslated 'religion,' *deen* encompasses much more that the simple acts of worship, extending to include the Islamic manners and codes of conduct in business, politics, family and community interactions and responsibilities, and all arenas of human existence.

Dunia – Material things of this world

Emaan – Faith

Fard – Obligatory

Fatwa – Legal ruling

Fiqh – Literally 'knowledge,' the word '*fiqh*' is practically applied to mean knowledge of Islamic laws

Hadith – A tradition recording the words, actions, appearance, or implied consents of Muhammad ibn Abdullah ﷺ.

Halal – Permissible

Haj – The annual Muslim pilgrimage to Makkah.

Haram – Forbidden

Hijra – The Muslim migration from Makkah to Medina in July of the year 622 CE.

Ibada – Worship

Iblees – See Iblis

Iblis – The proper name of the *Shaitan*

Ibn – Son of.

Ihsaan – God-consciousness

Ijma – Consensus (of the scholars)

Ijtihad – Independent reasoning (in arriving at a judgement)

Imam – Leader of the prayer, being the one who goes out in front of the congregation.

Imaan – Faith

Madhhab – School of legal thought

Makkah – (aka Mecca, Bakka, Becca, Baca) -- The holy city to which Muslims make pilgrimage. The Kaba, to which Muslims direct prayers, and the well of Zam-Zam is contained in the central, sacred mosque.

Mecca – See Makkah.

Nawafil – Supererogatory, or nonobligatory

Rakat – Interval of prayer

Sahaba – The companions of the prophet Muhammadﷺ.

Sahabi – Plural of *sahaba*

Salaf – The pious predecessors, referring to the first three generations following the messengership of Muhammadﷺ.

Salat – Prayer

Saum – Fasting

Shahada – Testimony of Islamic faith

Shaitan -- Satan

Shari'a – Islamic law

Shayateen – Evil jinn, or devils

Shirk – Violation of *tawheed* (Islamic monotheism)

Sunni – Orthodox sect of Islam, accounting for 95% of all Muslims.

Surah – Chapter of the Holy Qur'an.

Tariqa – Path (usually referring to a Sufi path, or order)

Tawbah – Repentance

Tawheed – Islamic monotheism.

Ulema – The body of Islamic scholars

Ummah – Nation

Umrah – *Nawafil* pilgrimage to Makkah

Zakat – The poor-due incumbent upon Muslims.